Hesler, Alexander
Galena, Illinois, 1852
Daguerreotype, 166 x 216mm.
Lent by the Iconographic Collections,
State Historical Society of Wisconsin,
Madison, Wisconsin.

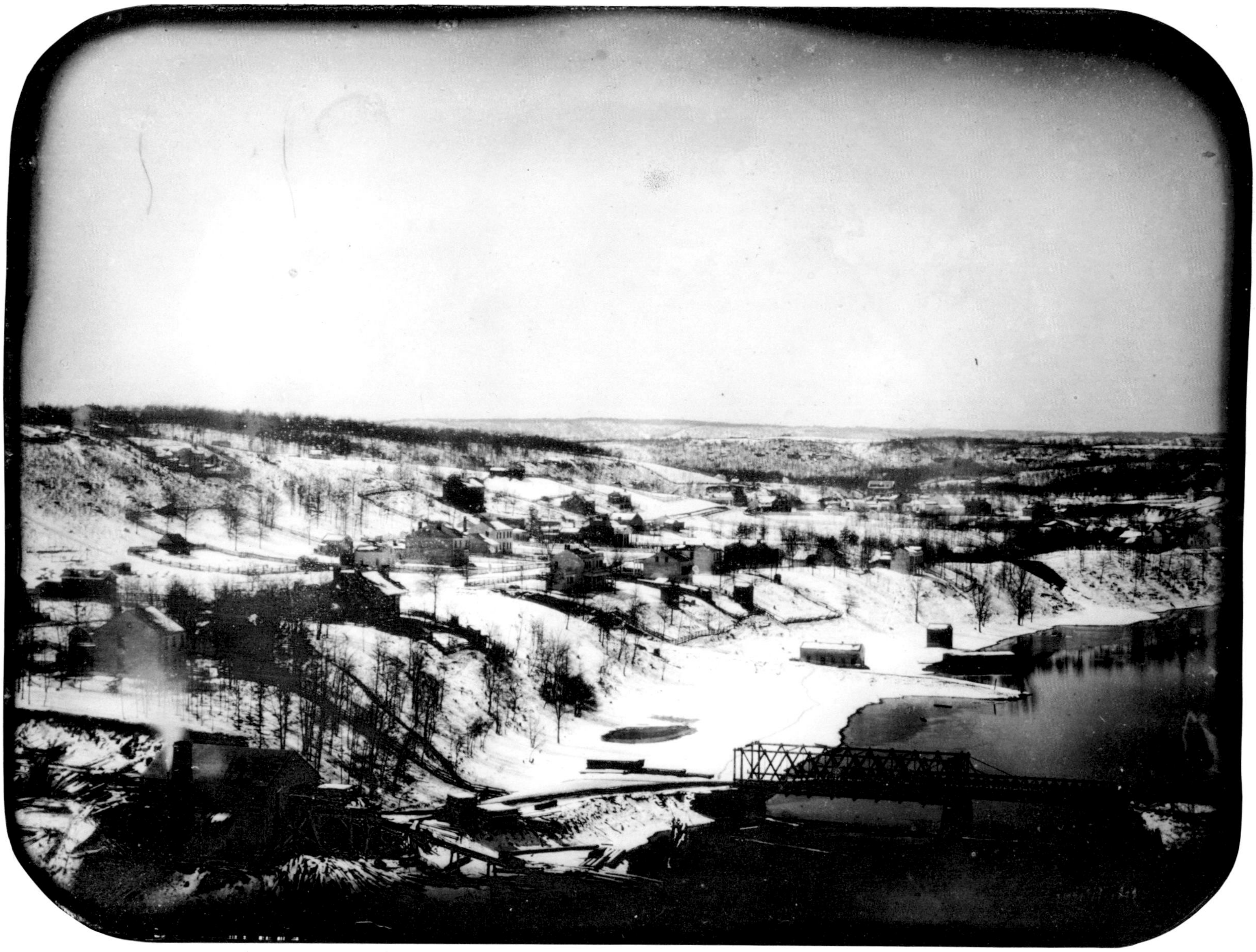

The Art Institute of Chicago

AN OPEN LAND: PHOTOGRAPHS

Rhondal McKinney
Curator

Victoria Post Ranney
Editor

Open Lands Project in association
with the Art Institute of Chicago
and Aperture, Inc.

OF THE MIDWEST, 1852-1982

Cundill, Will
South Dakota (Girl in Hay Stack), 1915
silver gelatin print, 125 x 175mm.
Modern print by J. Ceronie, Dennett,
Muessig & Associates from a negative
in the collection of the Iowa State
Historical Society, Iowa City, Iowa.
Lent by Open Lands Project of Chicago.

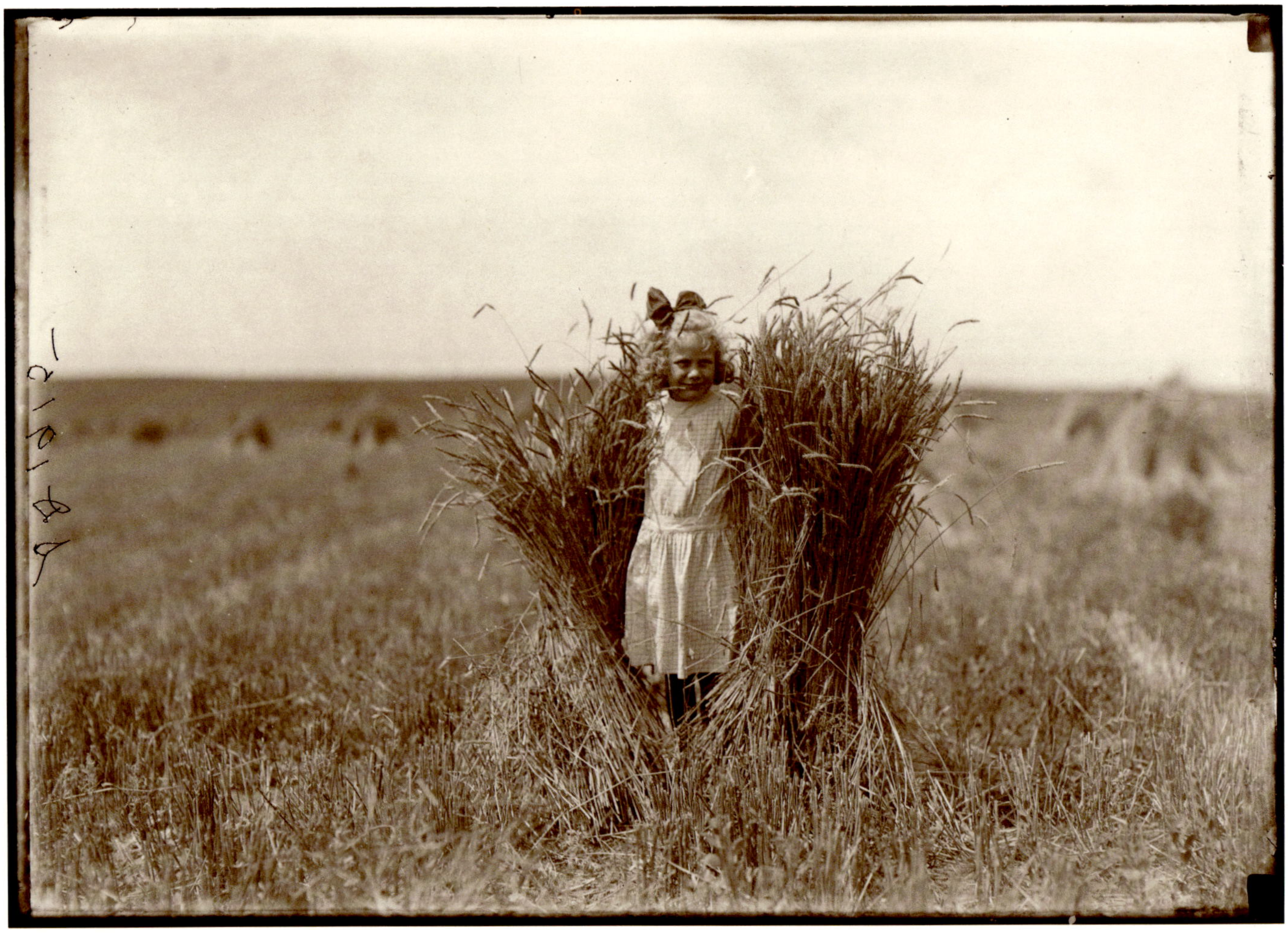

FOREWORD

Open Lands Project has been active in the area of land conservation since 1963. We have learned during our first twenty years that one of the greatest obstacles to conservation in the Midwest is the negative perception by many Midwesterners of their own land. Because this landscape offers neither purple mountains' majesty nor pounding surf it is somehow deemed less worthy of preservation.

Popular opinion about the esthetic value of landscape is led to a large degree by photographers, artists, poets and other creative imagists. There is a long and robust tradition of landscape art in the Midwest. It is a tradition that has produced a great many beautiful and compelling works. That the popular view of Midwest landscape should be in such opposition to the views expressed by our photographers, poets and artists could mean only that the general population is too little aware of their works. The purpose of this exhibition and catalogue is to bring some of these works to the public, providing the first-ever survey of landscape photography in the Midwest. It is our hope that by providing Midwesterners the opportunity to see their land as these artist have seen it, we will foster in people an increased appreciation.

This program has been under the direction of a committee of Open Lands Project whose members are:

Louise B. Young, Chair
Jacques Baruch
Stephen F. Christy
George Overton
Victoria Post Ranney
Jeffrey R. Short, Jr.
David Travis

Open Lands Project is grateful to these individuals for the many and various contributions they made to this effort.

Special thanks must go to George Overton. The idea of this program started with him and was spread by him in the early days. More than once it was the eloquence of his ardor that kept this program moving and provided it direction.

Special thanks also go to Louise B. Young for her steady and effective leadership of the committee, for forging this exhibition and catalogue from sometimes scattered resources and the talents of many people.

We thank David Travis, Curator Department of Photography at the Art Institute of Chicago, for the good guidance he gave to this effort. We also thank his staff, Deborah Frumkin, James Iska, Douglas Severson and Nancy Hamel for the invaluable assistance they gave. We are happy and proud to be associated with the Art Institute of Chicago in the production of this program.

We are indebted to Melissa M. Cain for the literature search which provided poems reproduced here, and readings on the Midwest landscape.

Rhondal McKinney is the one who has labored longest and hardest, first traveling around the country to find the photographs and then to orchestrate the final products. His good humor, persistence and great talent was our good fortune to discover and be associated with.

Funding for this program was provided by grants from:

Jacques Baruch
Illinois Humanities Council and the
National Endowment for the Humanities
Leslie Fund, Inc.
Ferd Kramer
Chauncey and Marion Deering McCormick Foundation
Mrs. C. Phillip Miller
George Overton
Marion Parry
Jeffrey R. Short, Jr.
Woods Charitable Fund, Inc.
Louise B. Young

Open Lands Project expresses deep gratitude to these grantors. Without their generous support this program would not have been possible.

Finally, special thanks go to the photographers and writers who allowed us to display and reproduce their works, and to the institutions and individuals who loaned photographs from their collections.

Arthur W. Berry,
President, Open Lands Project

Judith M. Stockdale
Executive Director, Open Lands Project

SEARCHING FOR LANDSCAPE IN PHOTOGRAPHS

by Rhondal McKinney

For twelve months during 1982 and 1983 I traveled around the Midwest looking for photographs to use in this exhibit and book. I went to historical societies, to government archives and met with many photographers. I came to this project with a background as a photographer and none as curator or historian. For several years I had photographed rural landscape in the Midwest and the working methods I had thus acquired were the ones I brought with me to this new project. Traveling from place to place sorting through piles of photographs, trying to decide which ones to set aside for use here was a process much like traveling around the countryside looking over the landscape, trying to decide where to stop and photograph.

I have always worked in or near the classical tradition of documentarists, using the camera in more or less straightforward ways. My background is small town, Midwestern and enough Calvinist that my tendency is to offer restriction to my hunches. Things have their limits. An unfettered intuition is crucial to the research of ideas but the intuition roams most freely over familiar territories. I was originally trained as a scientist and, although I am nowadays researching fictions instead of facts, I continue to work in my old style. The documentarian stylist strives for anonymity of voice and discipline of method—devices he uses to make his fictions convincing. No voice is really anonymous and the artist knows that intelligence comes to his work, if at all, by its own devious way, quite regardless of any stylized discipline.

When I was a child I spent a lot of time with my father going around the countryside in his pickup truck. My father was a fisherman and a quail hunter. We might have been on our way to the river to run his nets or driving around looking for evidence of quail but most of the time I didn't know where we were going. While we toured the countryside my father always chewed tobacco and therefore rarely spoke. The cab of that truck had been so dusty for so long that the dust now clung to the floorboard, the dash, everywhere, like hide. Soda bottles banged together under the seat. God only knew how many were under there. As we bumped along dirt roads past fields of clover and alfalfa, corn and wheat, past orchards and pastures and hardwood groves my father's eyes moved constantly back and forth across the view. He had a thirst for the look of the land. I remember at first wondering what it was that he was always looking at. At some point, though, I stopped wondering and started looking myself and eventually I learned to see what he saw, to love what he loved.

I was a photographer for several years before I came to photograph landscape. Having lived in this landscape all my life, my feelings about it were strong. The camera is an ungainly device at first. I felt some reluctance, I suppose, to turn it toward private realms. But one day I was driving with my wife and we pulled off the highway for a closer look at an old church we had glimpsed. While we were looking at the church a storm threatened and we got into the car and were hurrying back to the highway when I pulled over to watch the storm move in. The clouds were very dark and the field before me was of black mud. A strip of light at the horizon silhouetted distant trees and farm buildings. The clouds were spectacular. I remember how pure was the joy I felt during the few moments I spent setting up the camera, making the exposure, putting the camera away. Later in the darkroom when I saw the photograph the joy returned.

On another day I was driving to a nearby town when I found myself on an elevated roadway looking down on a recently planted field of corn. It was early in the day and the sun's heat drove moisture from the ground to hang in the air. The light was softened by this mist and the rows of new corn plants stretched and crisscrossed over the earth, revealing a subtle rise and fall of the land. In the near distance a white farm building glowed. I made an exposure and decided to cancel my trip, instead to spend the morning driving around the countryside looking for pictures.

Within a short while I was totally involved in landscape work, feeling none of the reluctance I had felt earlier. My interest in the landscape was apart from that of the conservationist or agriculturist or geologist. It was the photograph that was the important thing to me. I wanted these photographs to be about the private experience of the individual with the landscape, with the message it conveys about beauty, nurture, geologic time, spirituality. Rather than make photographs that were representations of the land, I wanted to make photographs that themselves provided a source of direct experience with landscape.

"I can't see this as a beautiful landscape," a friend once said to me upon viewing some of my photographs. "These cultivated fields are just food factories and I can't accept them as beautiful."

"For most of us this landscape is the natural landscape," I said.

"Much of what we know about nature and beauty is going to come from our experience with this landscape."

"Maybe you can say 'beauty' but not 'nature'. You can't call it natural without robbing the word of its meaning. It's man-made."

"Well, it is man-altered, not man-made. But even the alterations might be considered natural in some ways. It might be considered natural for people to take their living from the land. Doing it with backhoes and combines is no less natural than doing it with pointed sticks."

"It is different," she said. "The land is left unnatural, it isn't beautiful in the natural sense."

I will admit that the degree to which this landscape has been altered sometimes saddens me. Sometimes I want to make a photograph that suggests the absence of man. A wheat field under dim light might look like a wild prairie. I might shift the camera to one side a little and cut out a telephone pole. But at other times the man-made alterations are the most beautiful elements of the photographs: the rows of cultivated fields, the sweep of a high tension wire along the horizon. One cannot say what might cause the spirit to soar. I have marveled at the beauty of photographs of shopping centers, the greatest blight on our landscape. The cosmetic changes people have brought to the land seem even trivial at times, certainly by comparison to the changes nature has brought. Carl Sandburg wrote in his poem "Prairie":

I am here when the cities are gone,
I am here before the cities come,
I nourished the lonely men on horseback,
I will keep the laughing men who ride iron,
I am dust of men.

"What are you taking a picture of?" A women asked me this one spring afternoon. I was standing on top of my truck with my camera and tripod and she had pulled her car alongside. It was a fine afternoon.

"Landscape," I said. I spread my arms to indicate what I meant. Before my camera stood only land, sky and horizon.

The women looked around in all directions and then back to me. "What landscape?" she asked.

What landscape. I wanted to say 'Well, if you saw the photograph you would understand.' Often beauty is more easily sensed in the photograph than in the real scene. The photograph abstracts from the real scene. Faced with this abstraction the viewer disarms, the message gets through. Not always, of course. But a few people have told me that they learned to see beauty in this landscape from looking at my pictures. Probably they would have seen it by themselves eventually. I do not expect photographs to change the minds of unwilling viewers.

Late on another spring day I was standing with my camera in a bean field waiting for the sun to drop a little lower in the sky. A pickup truck came down the road and stopped behind mine and a young farmer got out and started slowly toward me. This happens to me often and it is always a moment of some tension for me since I have been ordered away a few times. Most of the time, though, the farmers I encounter have enough understanding of what I am doing that they let me finish my work. This young farmer stopped about twenty yards away and watched me make some camera adjustments, go under the dark cloth and come out again. I spoke first. Sometimes I can head these guys off.

"I'm just waiting for the sun to get down a little, then I'm going to make a picture of this field."

The ground was falling away from me slightly and it rose again a few hundred yards away and the rows formed by the planter swooped toward a ridge at the far side of the field. About half way into the picture the land rose and fell again but this was very subtle. You can't see it except under certain lighting conditions and during certain stages of cultivation.

The farmer nodded and looked pleased. "I'll tell you," he said, "When the sun sits on that ridge over there is just about the best time of day for anything around here—picture taking, you name it." His voice had the pitch and tremor of emotion in it and I thought he would speak again but the throat is the organ of wisdom in Midwesterners and his choked off whatever else he would have said then. The farmer looked away and seemed embarrassed at having betrayed this emotion. Somehow the sting in his cheeks transferred to mine and I too was embarrassed. We stood in place a few moments longer; he finally turned.

"Well," was all he said as he began high-stepping over the rows of beans toward his truck.

A few minutes later I got the picture I wanted.

Hime, H.L.
The Prairie, on the Banks of the Red River, Looking South, September-October, 1858
albumen print, 133 x 170mm.
Lent by Notman Photographic Archives, McCord Museum, McGill University, Montreal, Quebec, Canada.

Hime, H.L.
Tents on the Prairie, West of the Settlement, September-October, 1858
albumen print, 133 x 170mm.
Lent by Notman Photographic Archives, McCord Museum, McGill University, Montreal, Quebec, Canada.

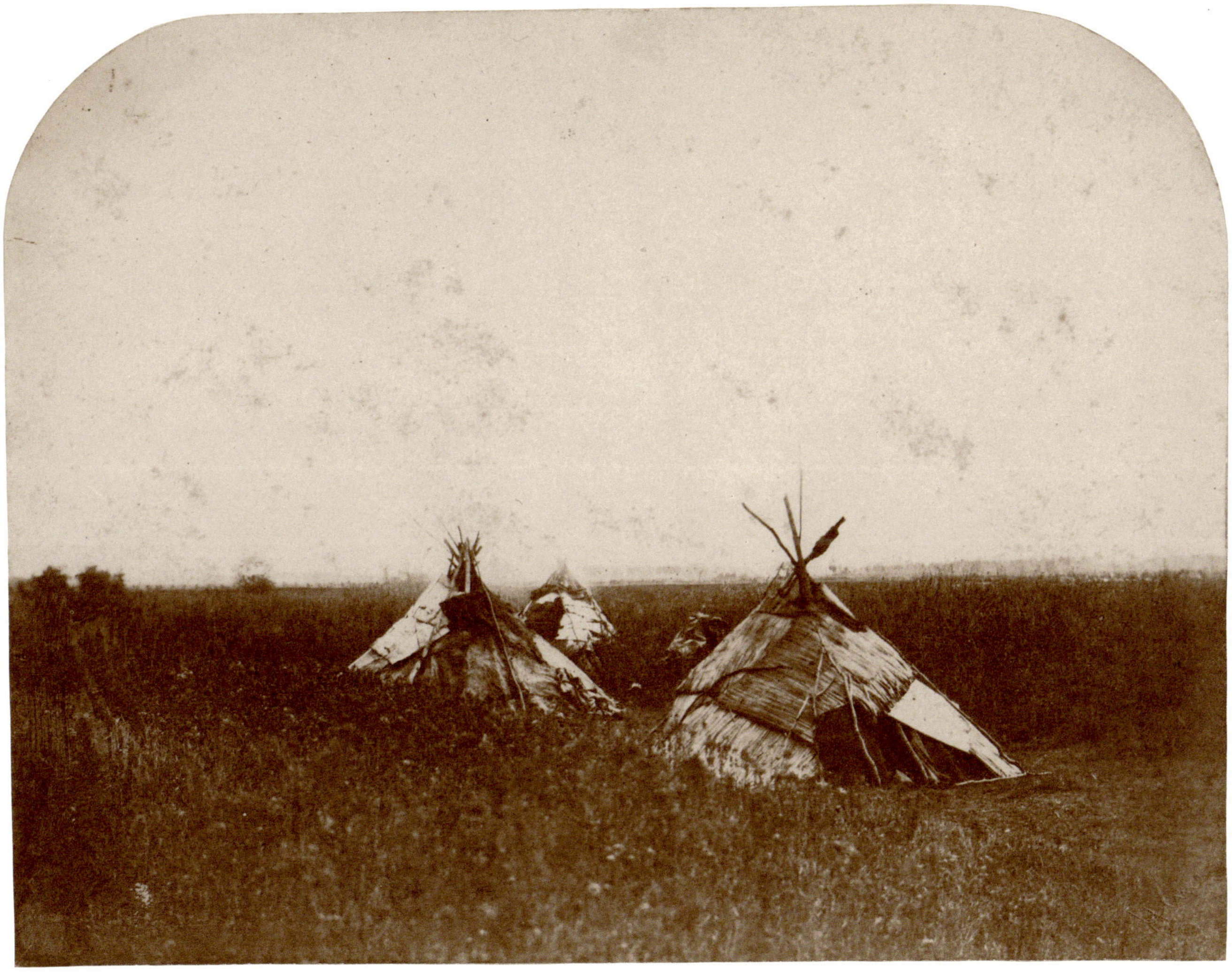

Gardner, Alexander
View Near Fort Harker, Kansas, 1867
albumen print, 149 x 202mm.
Lent by the Missouri Historical Society,
St. Louis, Missouri.

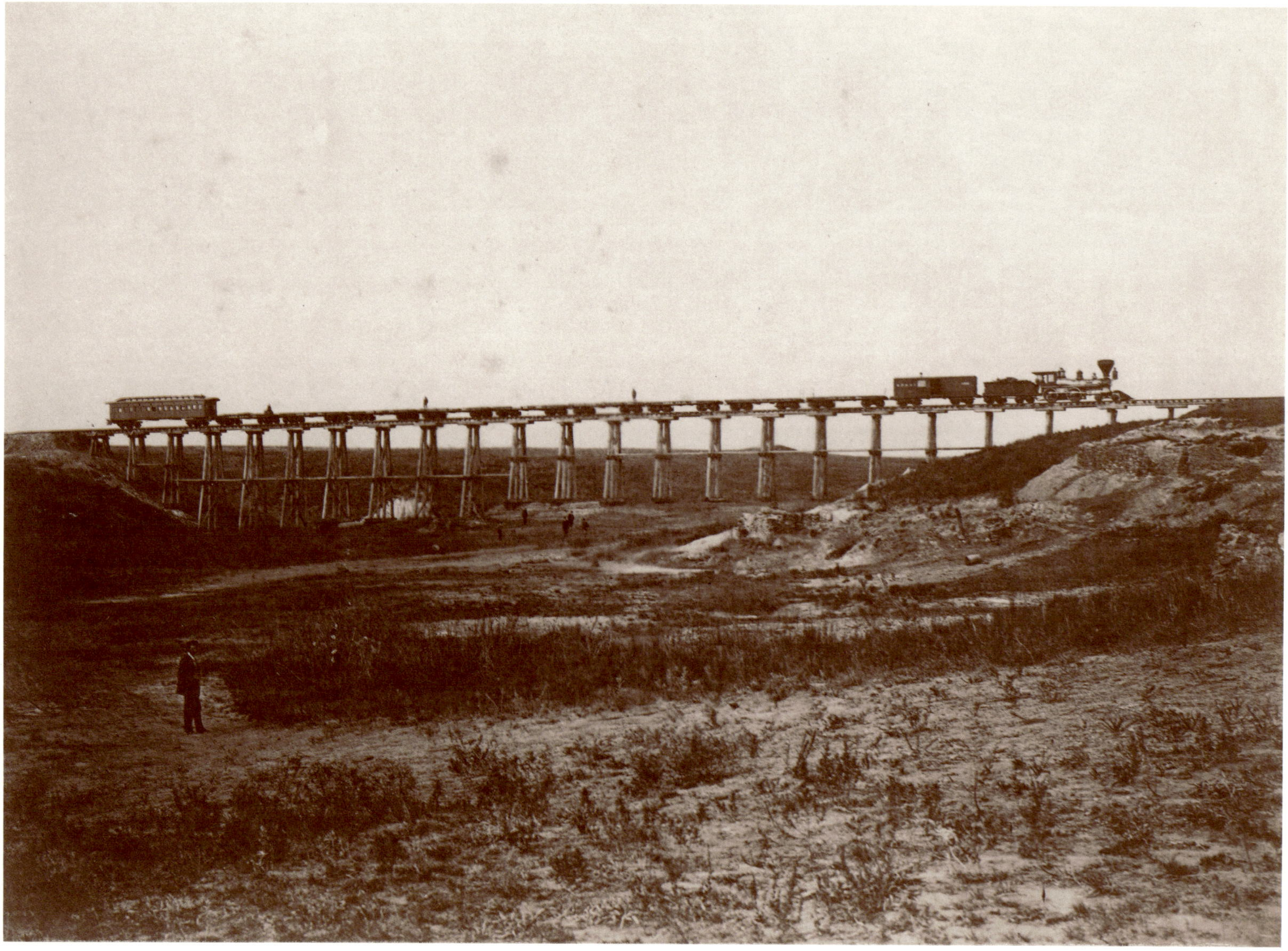

Gardner, Alexander
Overlooking Lawrence and the Kansas River, 1867
albumen print, 150 x 203mm.
Lent by the Missouri Historical Society, St. Louis, Missouri.

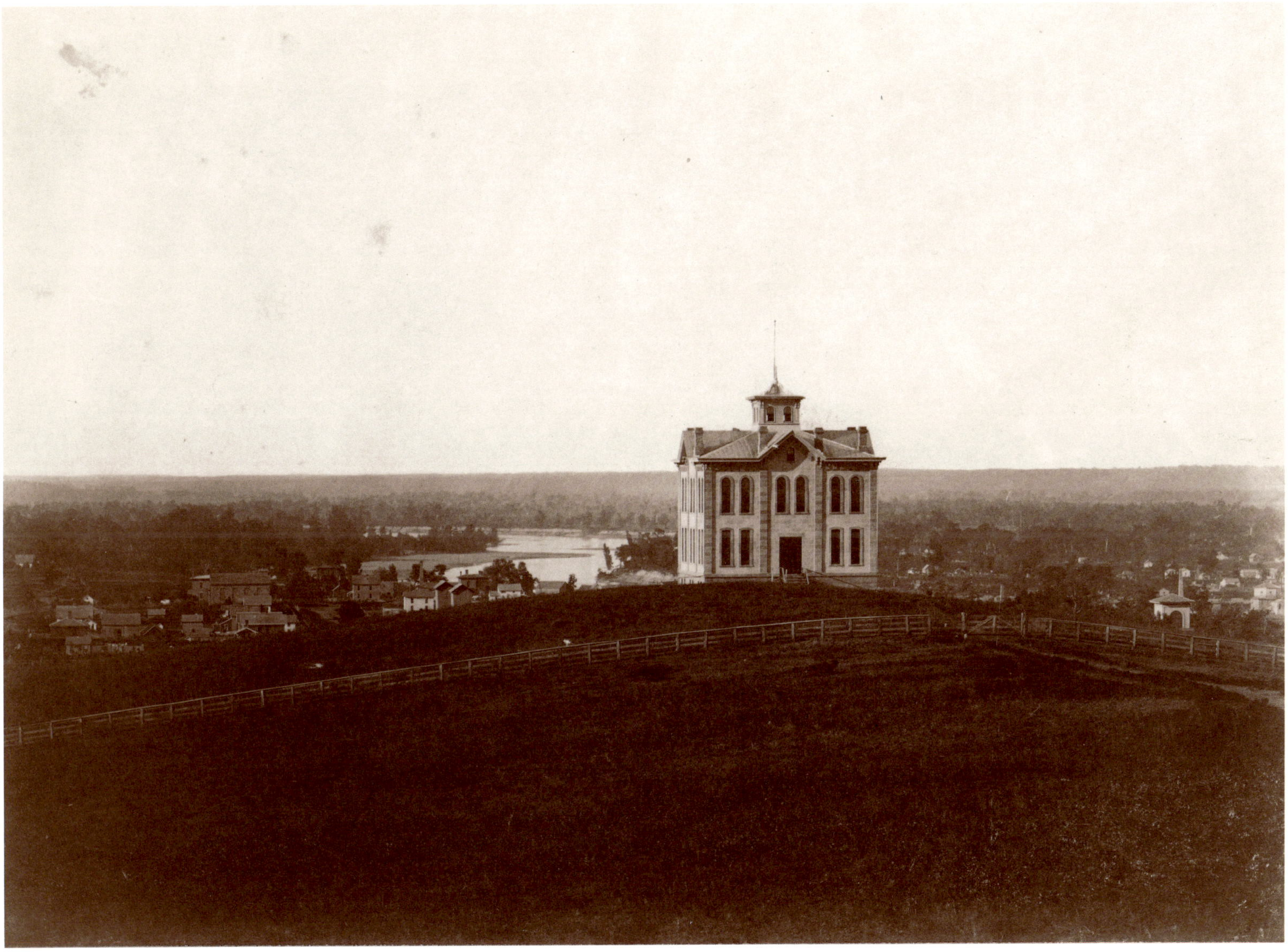

Dahl, Andrew
Workers with Farm Tools, c. 1873
(WHi (D31) 172)
albumen stereograph, 124 x 201mm.
Print by Elizabeth Chilsen and Lorraine Davis from a negative in the Iconographic Collections, State Historical Society of Wisconsin, Madison, Wisconsin, from paper provided by the Chicago Albumen Works.

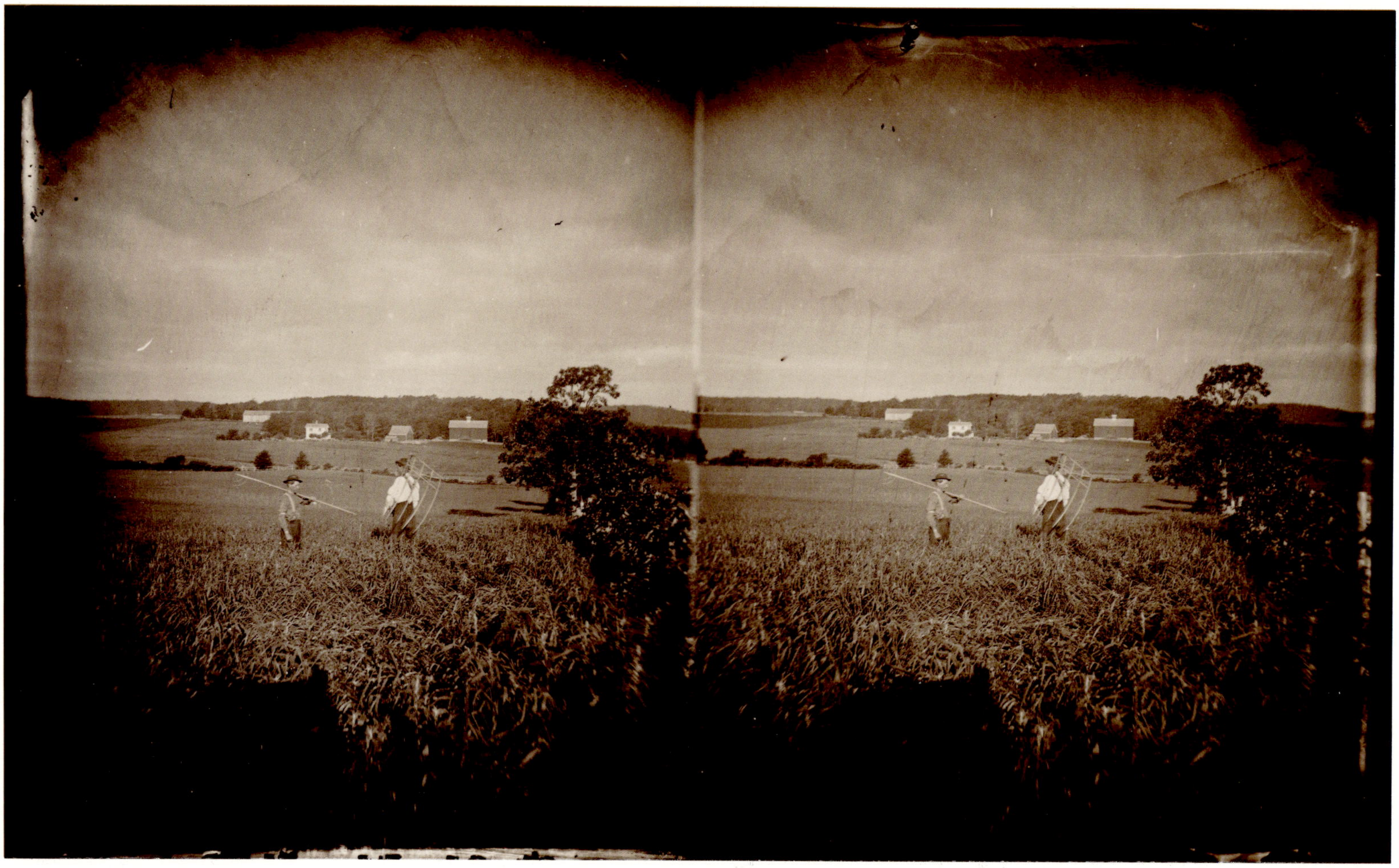

Dahl, Andrew
Workers with Farm Tools, Boy Facing Camera, c. 1873
(WHi (D31) 174)
albumen stereograph, 124 x 201mm.
Print by Elizabeth Chilsen and Lorraine Davis from a negative in the Iconographic Collections, State Historical Society of Wisconsin, Madison, Wisconsin, from paper provided by the Chicago Albumen Works.

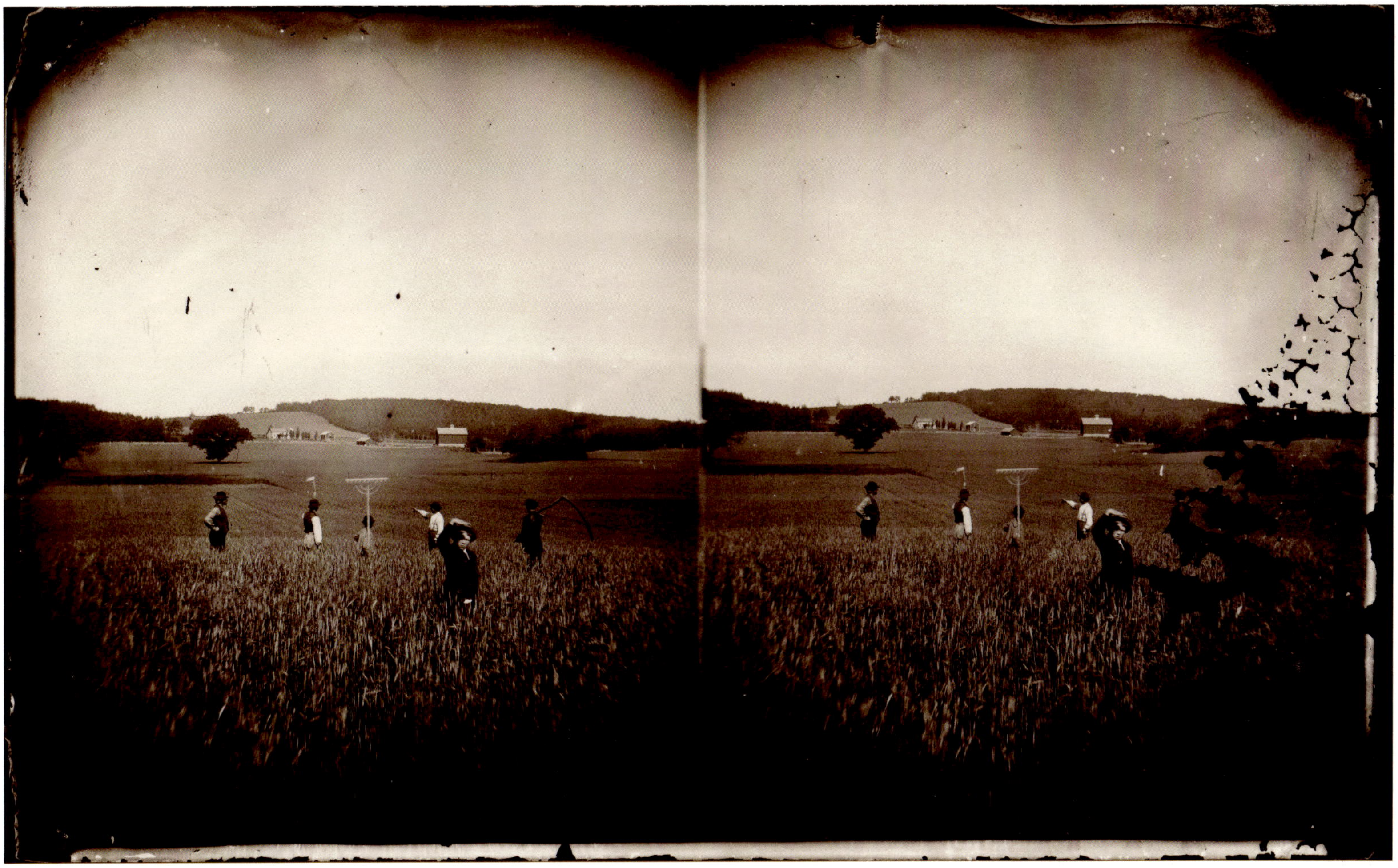

Robinson, F.N.
The Only Cyclone Ever Photographed (Miner County, South Dakota),
August 28, 1884
albumen print, 104 x 151mm.
Lent by the South Dakota State Historical Society, Pierre, South Dakota.

Lane, Frank
Fisherman, Reflection, c. 1896
silver gelatin print, 76 x 100mm.
Lent by the Momence (Illinois) Historical Society.

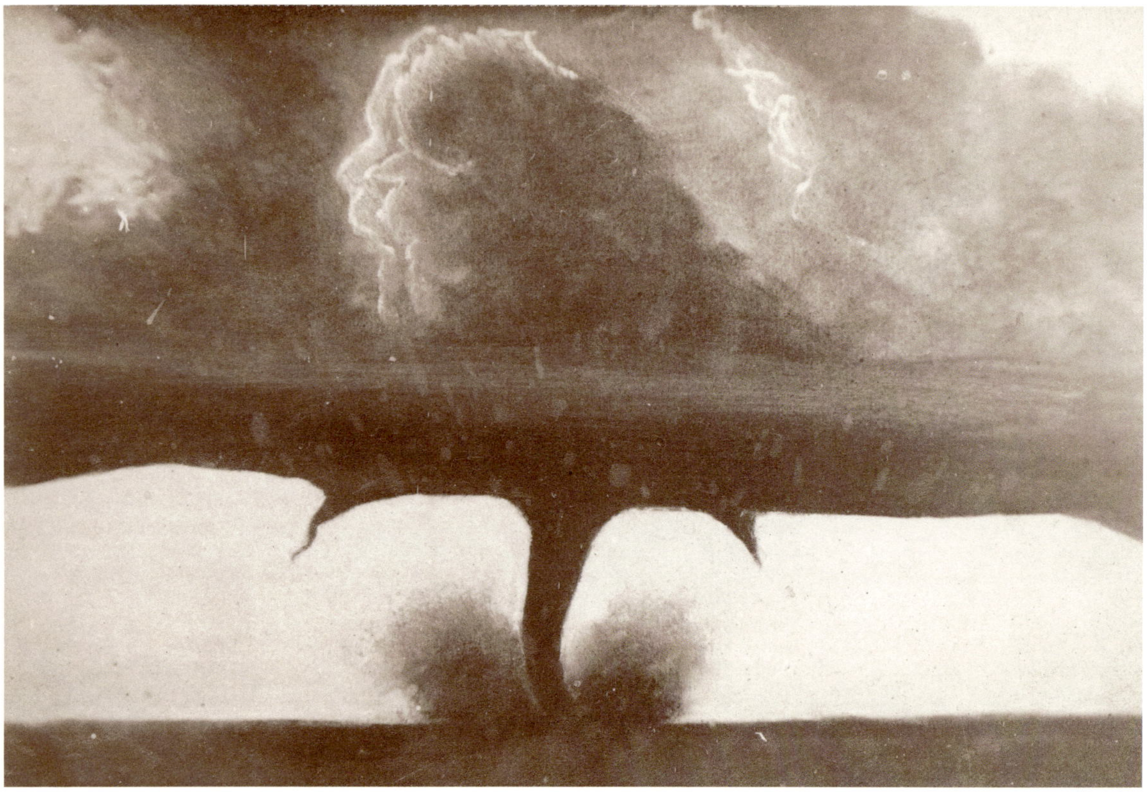

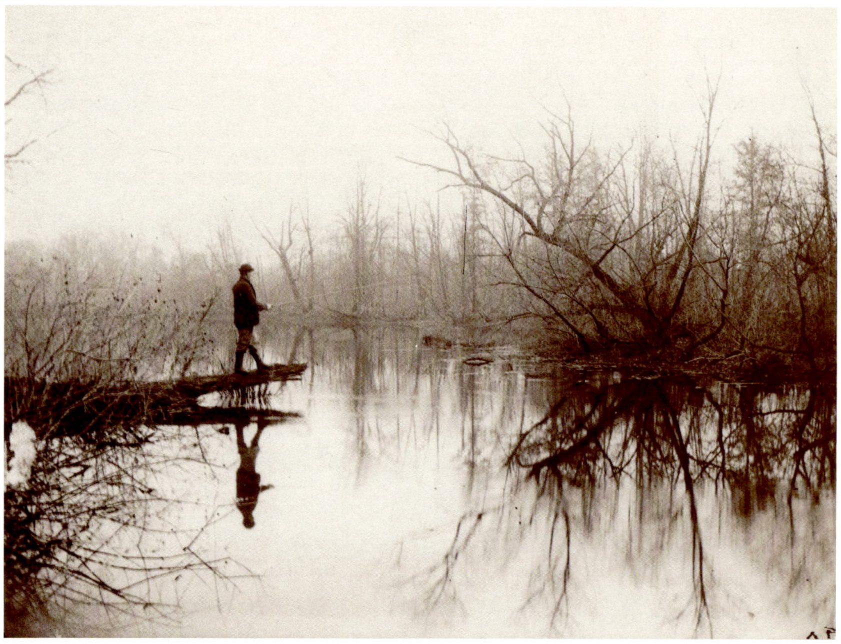

Fisher, Anna
Calhoun County, Illinois, c. 1903
silver gelatin print, 115 x 165mm.
Lent by Pike County Historical Society, Illinois.

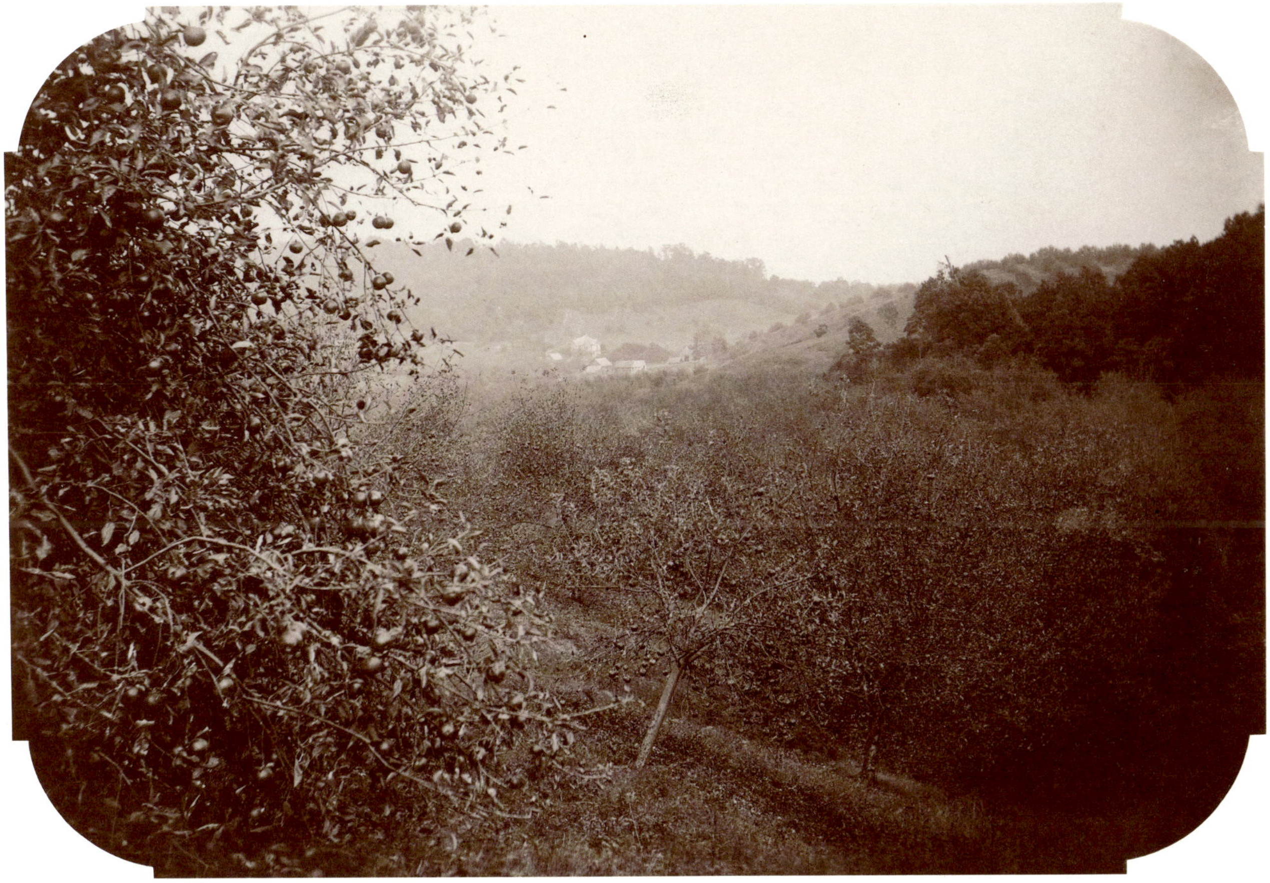

Johnson, W.D.
Man Sitting by Sink Hole (Kansas), 1897
silver gelatin print, 120 x 170mm.
Modern print by Rod Mettler from a
negative in the collection of the
U.S. Geological Survey. Lent by
Open Lands Project of Chicago.

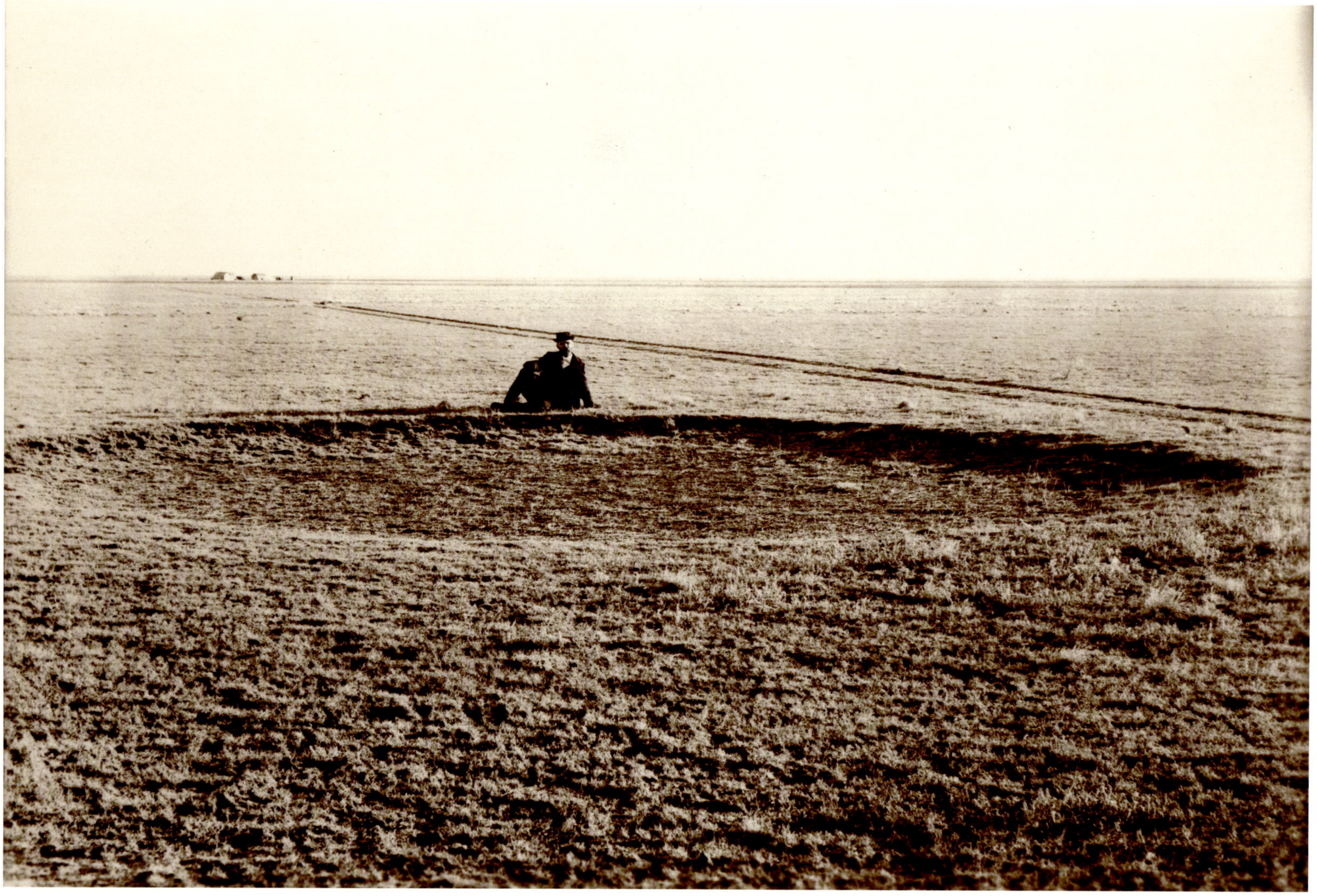

Hickman, C.A.
South Dakota Landscape with Children,
c. 1890
silver gelatin print, 52 x 176mm.
Lent by Robert Adams.

Anonymous
Two Hundred Twenty-Acre Field, Headed,
Stewart Valley, Saskatchewan, c. 1918
silver gelatin print, 62 x 168mm.
Lent by the Minnesota Historical Society,
St. Paul, Minnesota.

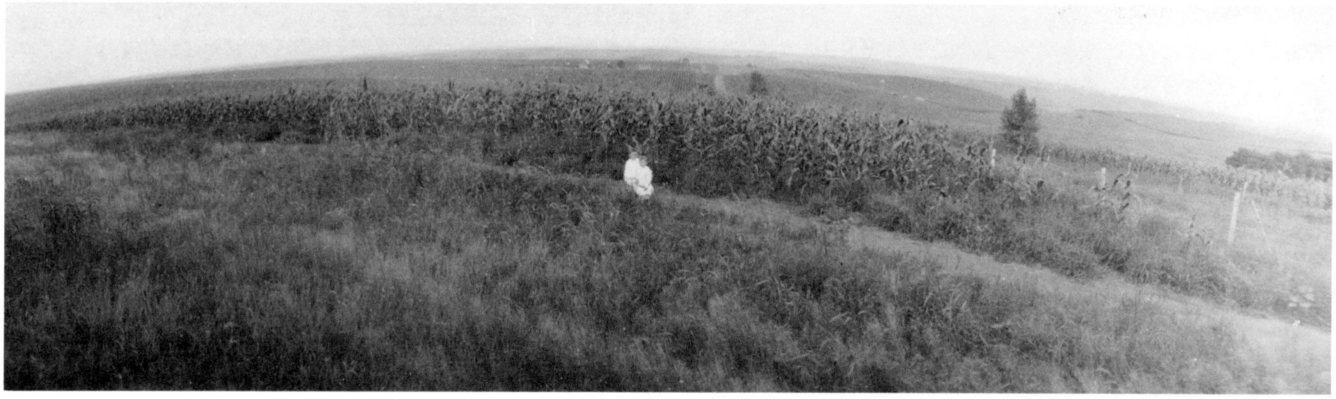

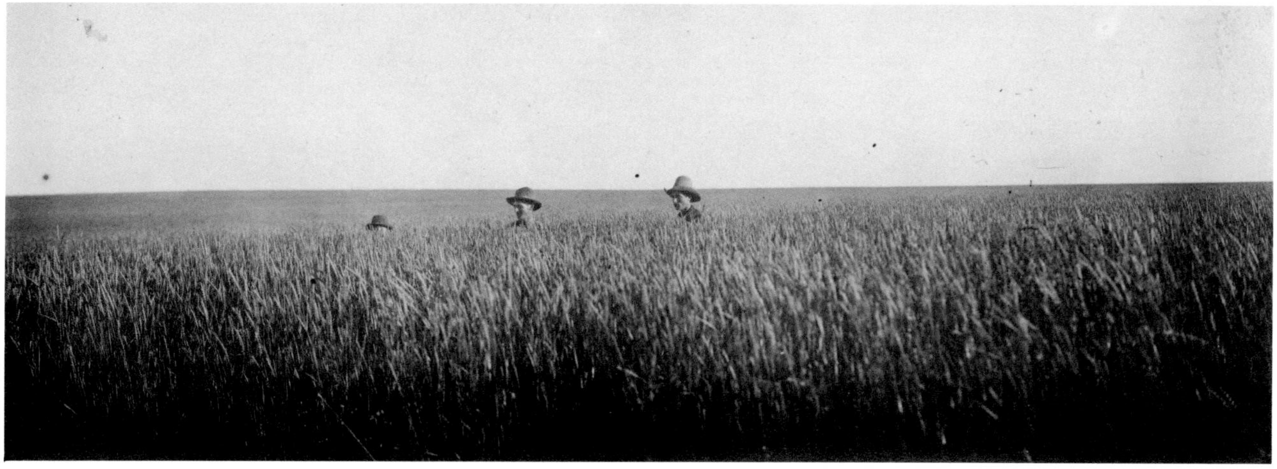

Gesell, Gerhard
Near Alma, Wisconsin, c. 1890
silver gelatin print, 188 x 246mm.
Lent by the Iconographic Collections,
State Historical Society of Wisconsin,
Madison, Wisconsin.

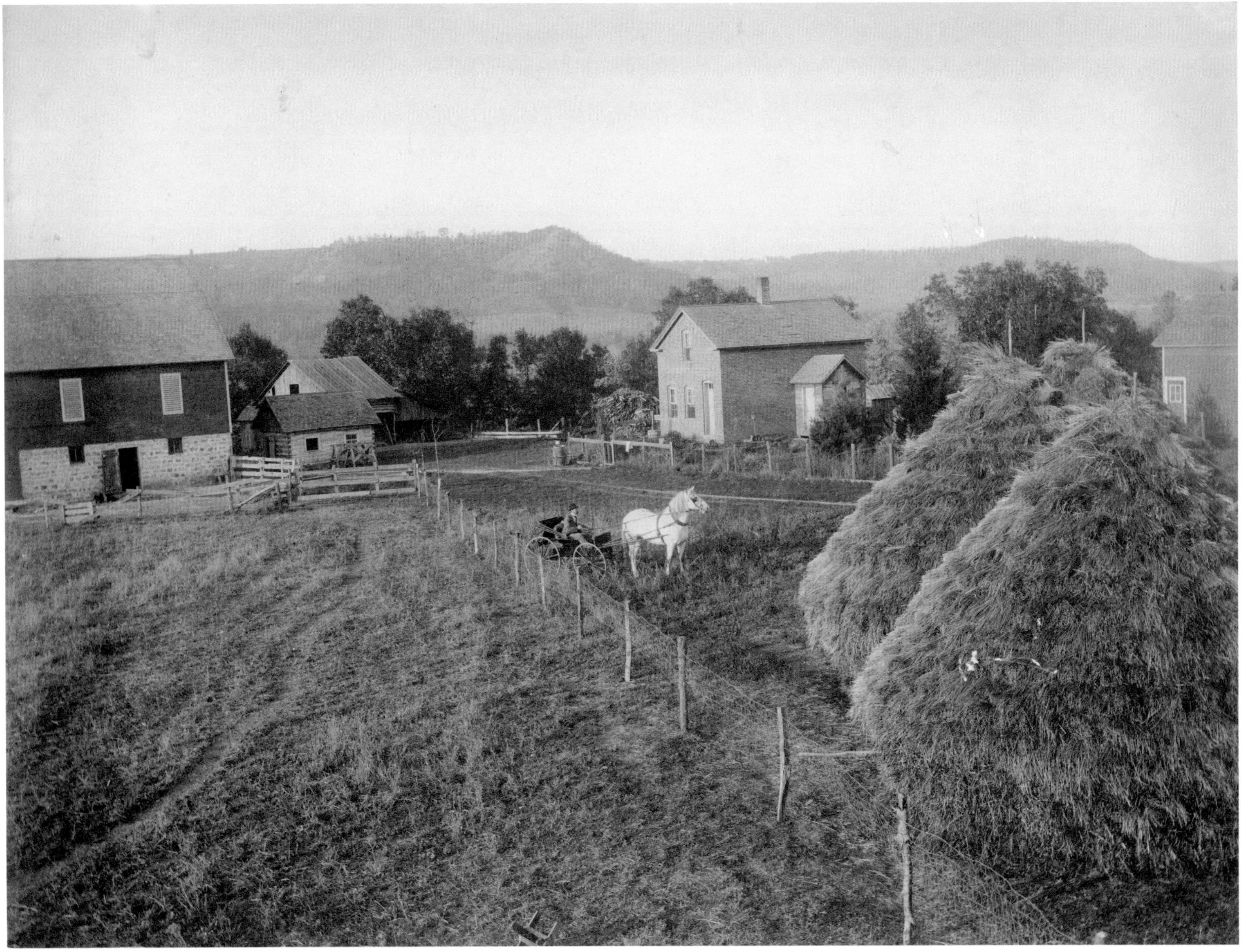

Ridgeway, Robert
Southern Illinois, Woman in White Dress,
c. 1885
silver gelatin print, 115 x 167mm.
Lent by the Chicago Academy of Sciences.

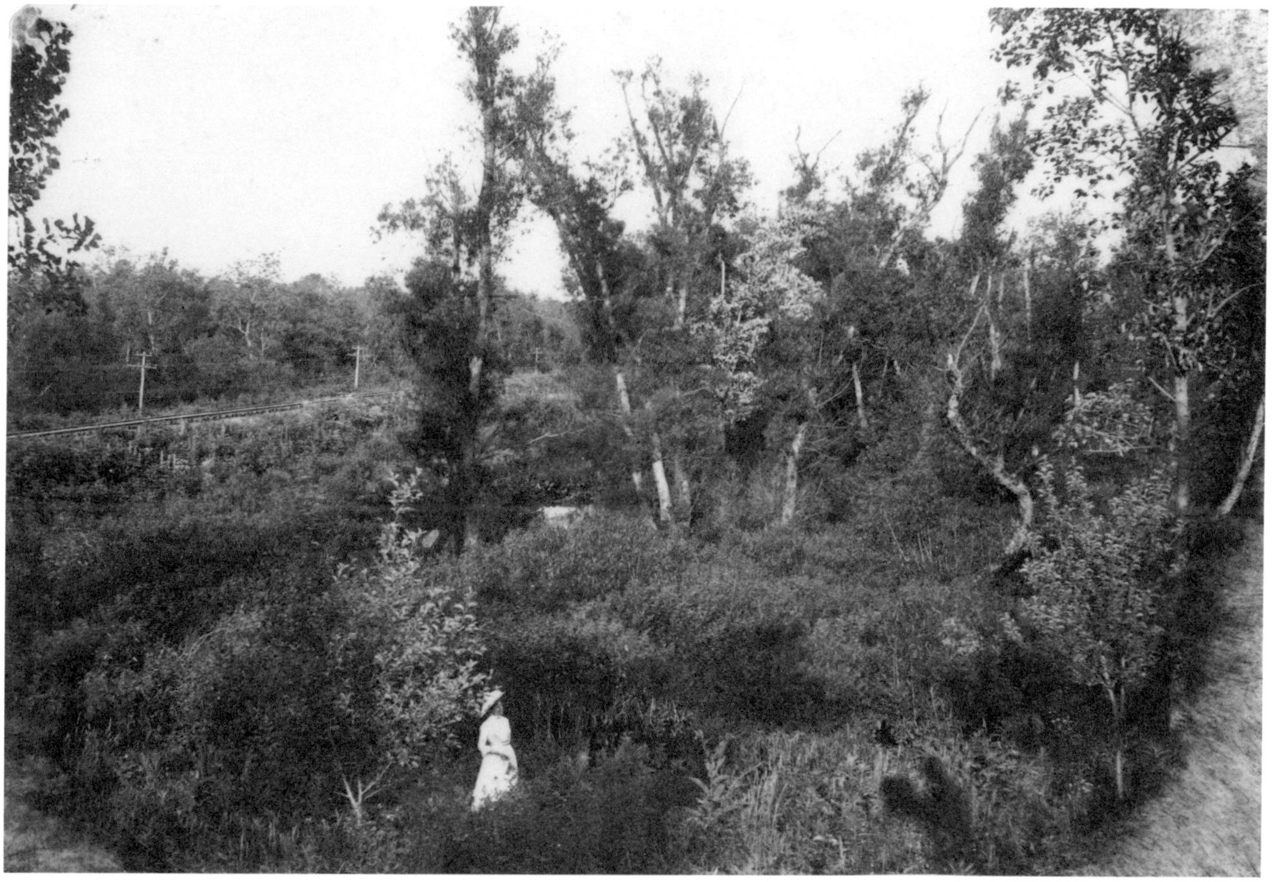

Midland

Under the great cold lakes, under the midmost
Parallel that Lisbon too lies under—
Vesuvius and Corinth, Ararat,
Peking and Chosen, yellow and blue seas
Enormous, then the redwoods, then high Denver—
Under the wet midnorth, under cool Canada,
Swings my own West, directionless; the temperate,
The tacit, the untold. There was I born,
There fed upon the dish of dreaming land
That feeds upon itself, forever sunk
From the far rim, from crust and outer taste,
Forever lost and pleased, as circling currents
Swim to themselves, renumbering Sargasso
Centuries a wind brings round the world.
There am I still, if no thought can escape
To edges from that soft and moving center,
That home, that floating grave of what would fly
Yet did not: my own boyhood, meditating
Unto no end, eternal where I was.

MARK VAN DOREN

Pennell, Joseph Judd
Tom Flannagan's Monument, 1898
silver gelatin print, 183 x 224mm.
Modern print by Jon Blumb
from a negative in the Kansas Collection,
University of Kansas, Lawrence, Kansas.
Lent by Open Lands Project of Chicago.

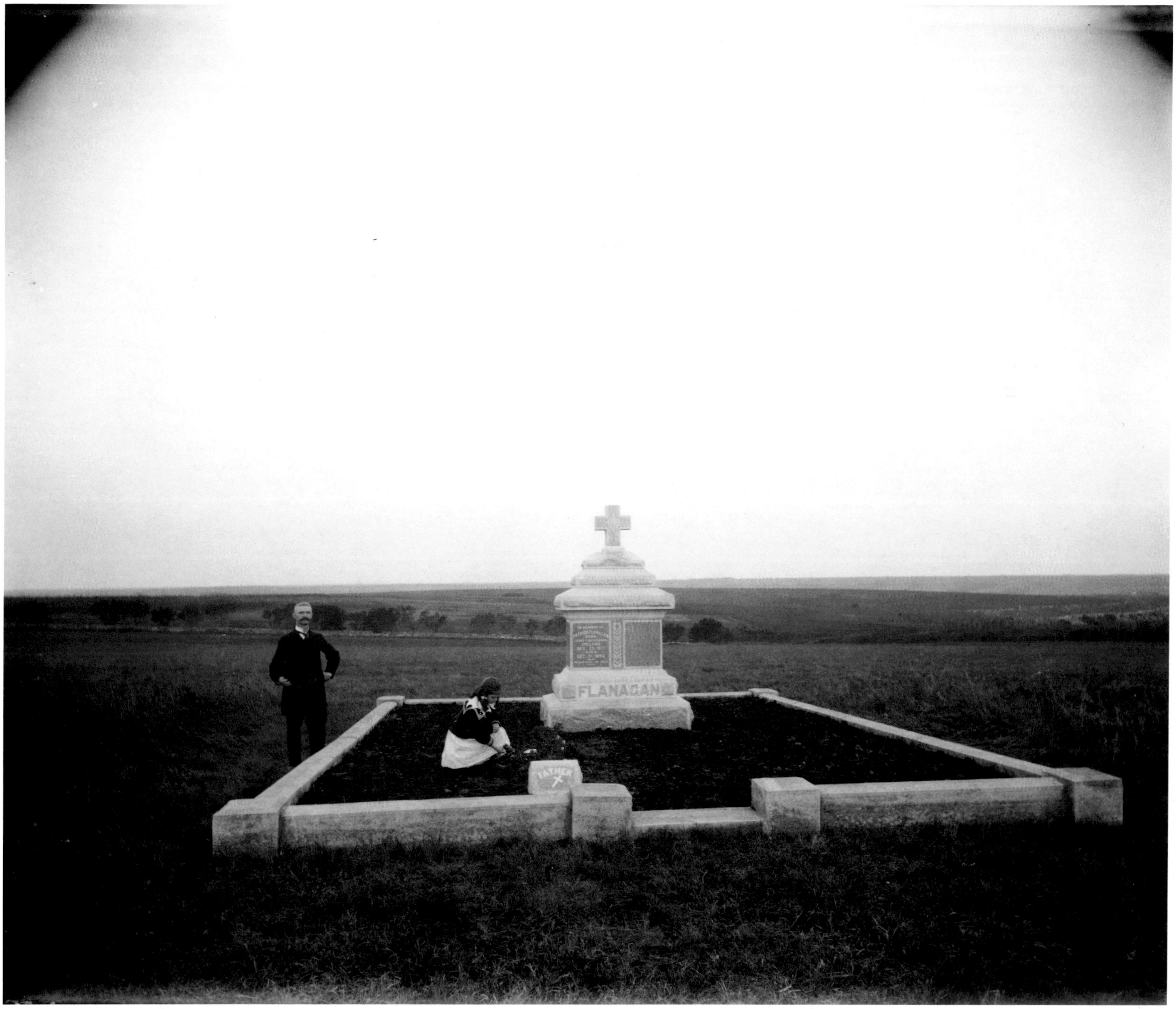

Persons, W.C.
Threshing Scene, c. 1920
silver gelatin print, 186 x 241mm.
Lent by the Missouri Historical Society,
St. Louis, Missouri.

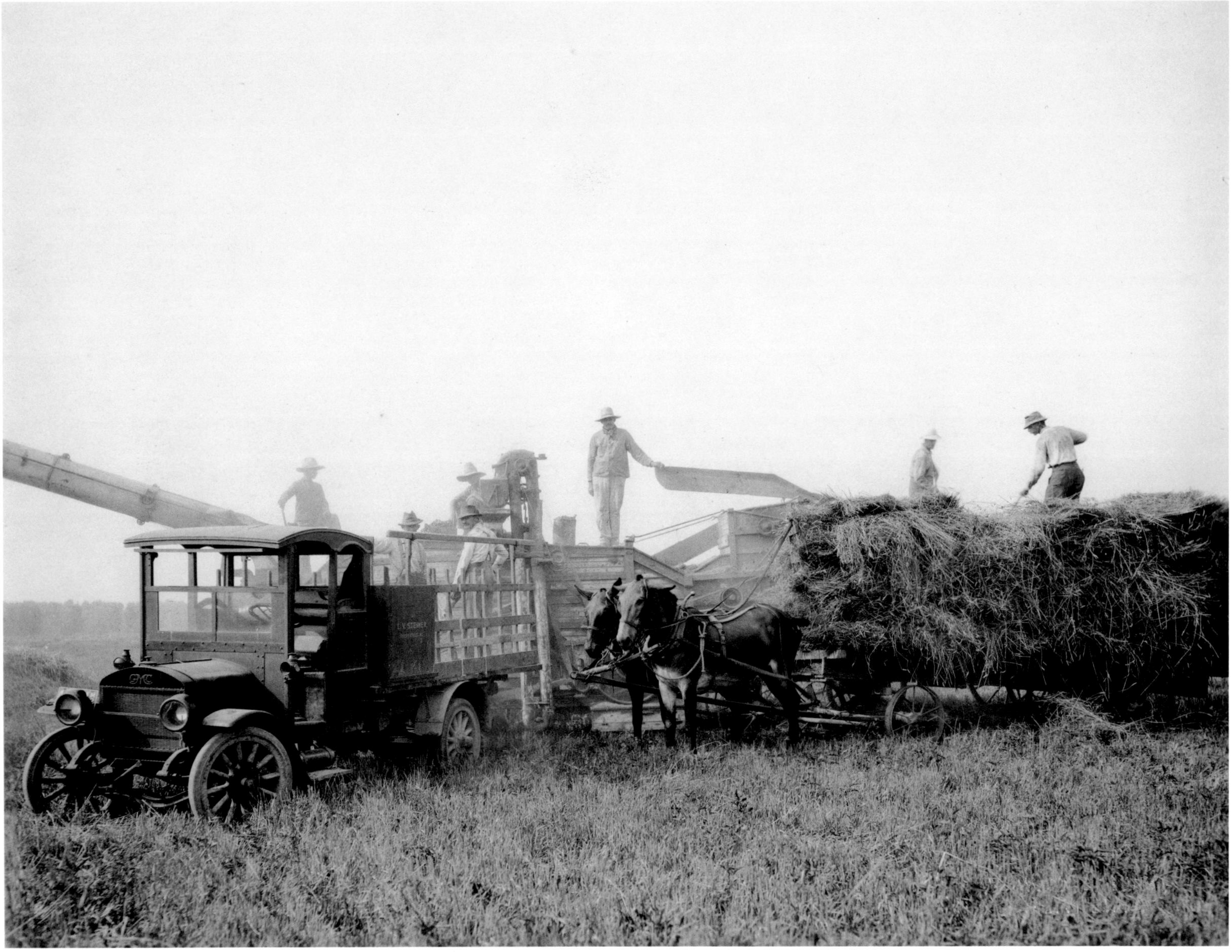

Allen, J.C.
Scene in Switzerland County, Indiana,
June 1922
silver gelatin print, 115 x 164mm.
Lent by J.C. Allen & Son, Inc.,
West Lafayette, Indiana.

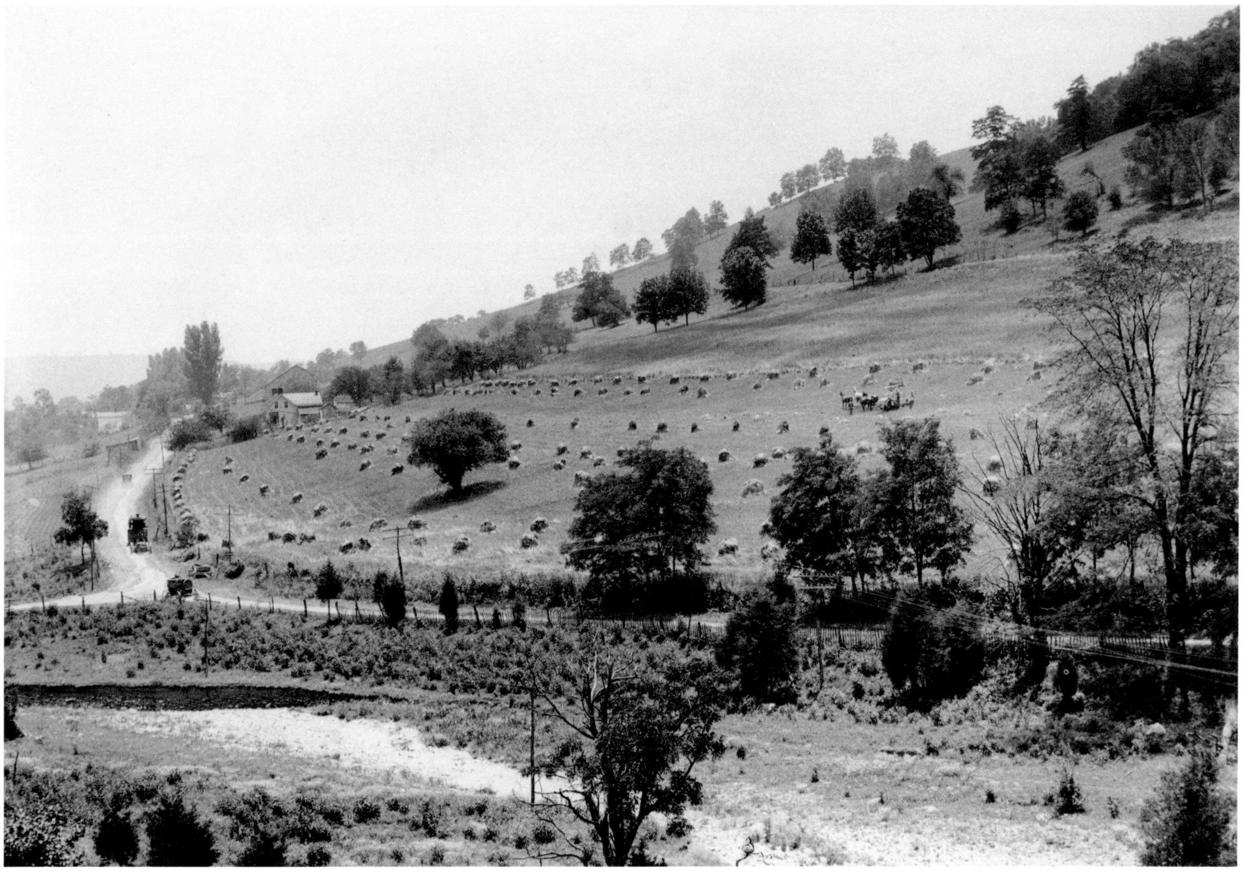

Allen, J.C.
Scene from Elevator
Near Earl Park, Indiana, July 1927
silver gelatin print, 115 x 164mm.
Lent by J.C. Allen & Son, Inc.,
West Lafayette, Indiana.

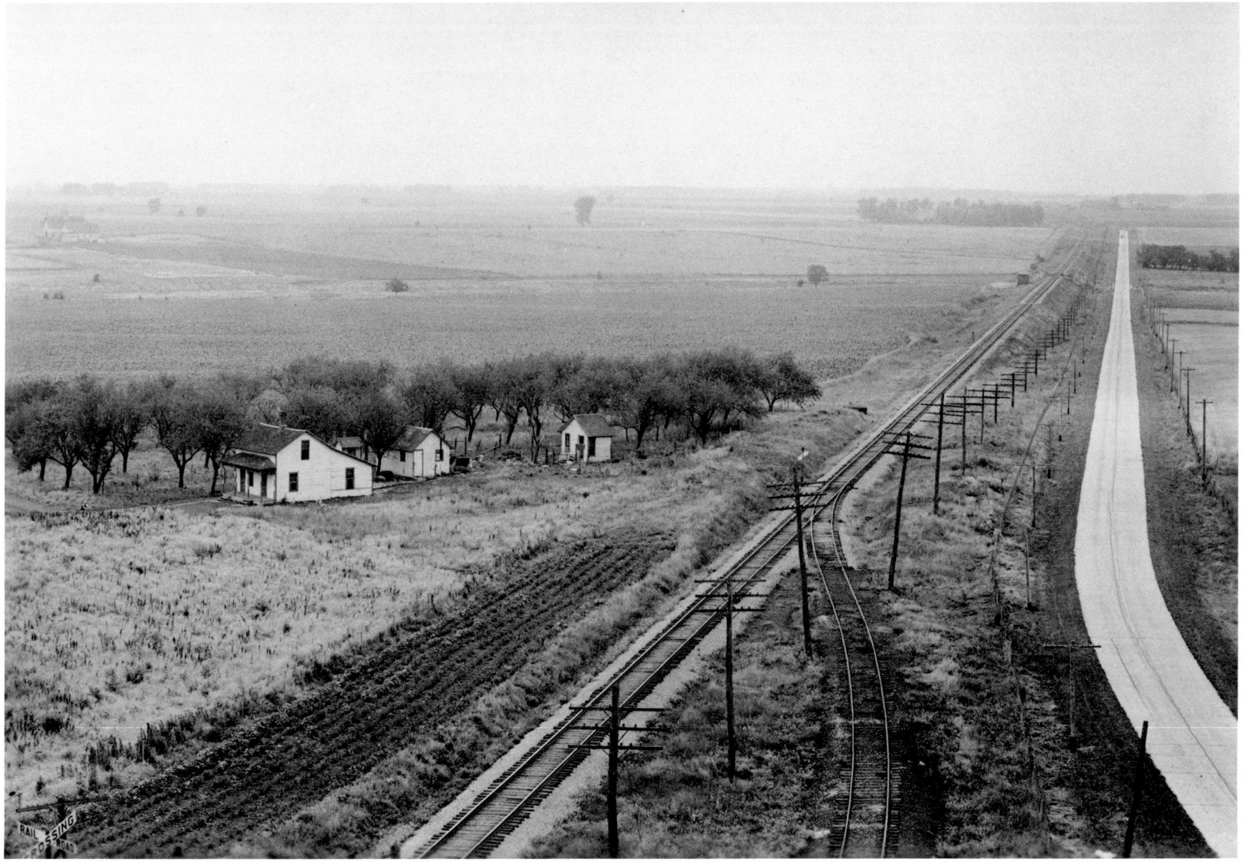

West of Chicago

Beneath these plains
Are the bones
Of small horses.
Invisible in the sunlight
The ghosts of dead Indians
Move over the land;
Searching for the ruined settlements
Seeking their scattered children.

In the quiet, neat towns
At night
The houses and small streets
Disappear in the darkness.
And again in the distance
You can hear
Or think you hear
The bare winds
Moving across the great plains.

JOHN DIMOFF

Anonymous
Man on Bluff, Mississippi River, 1930
silver gelatin print, 162 x 112mm.
Lent by Principia College, Elsah, Illinois.

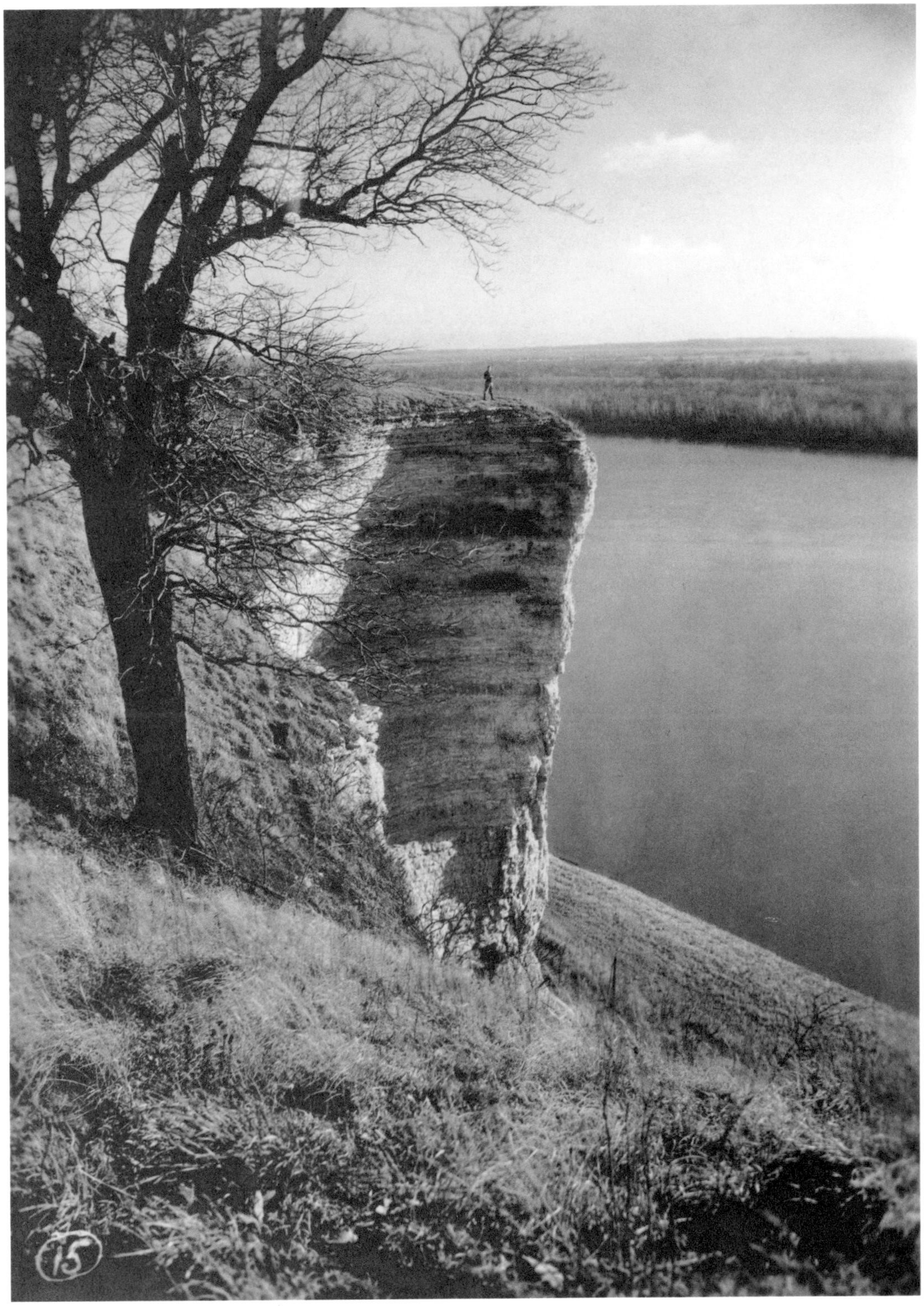

Sinsabaugh, Art
Midwest Landscape # 24, 1961
silver gelatin print, 67 x 490mm.
Lent by Edwynn Houk Gallery, Chicago.

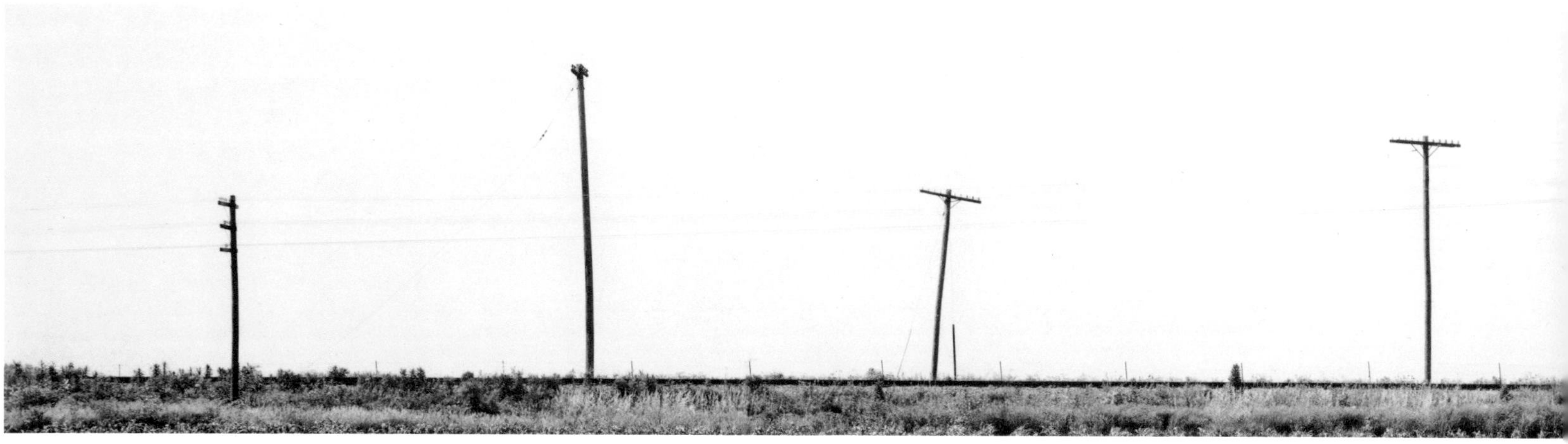

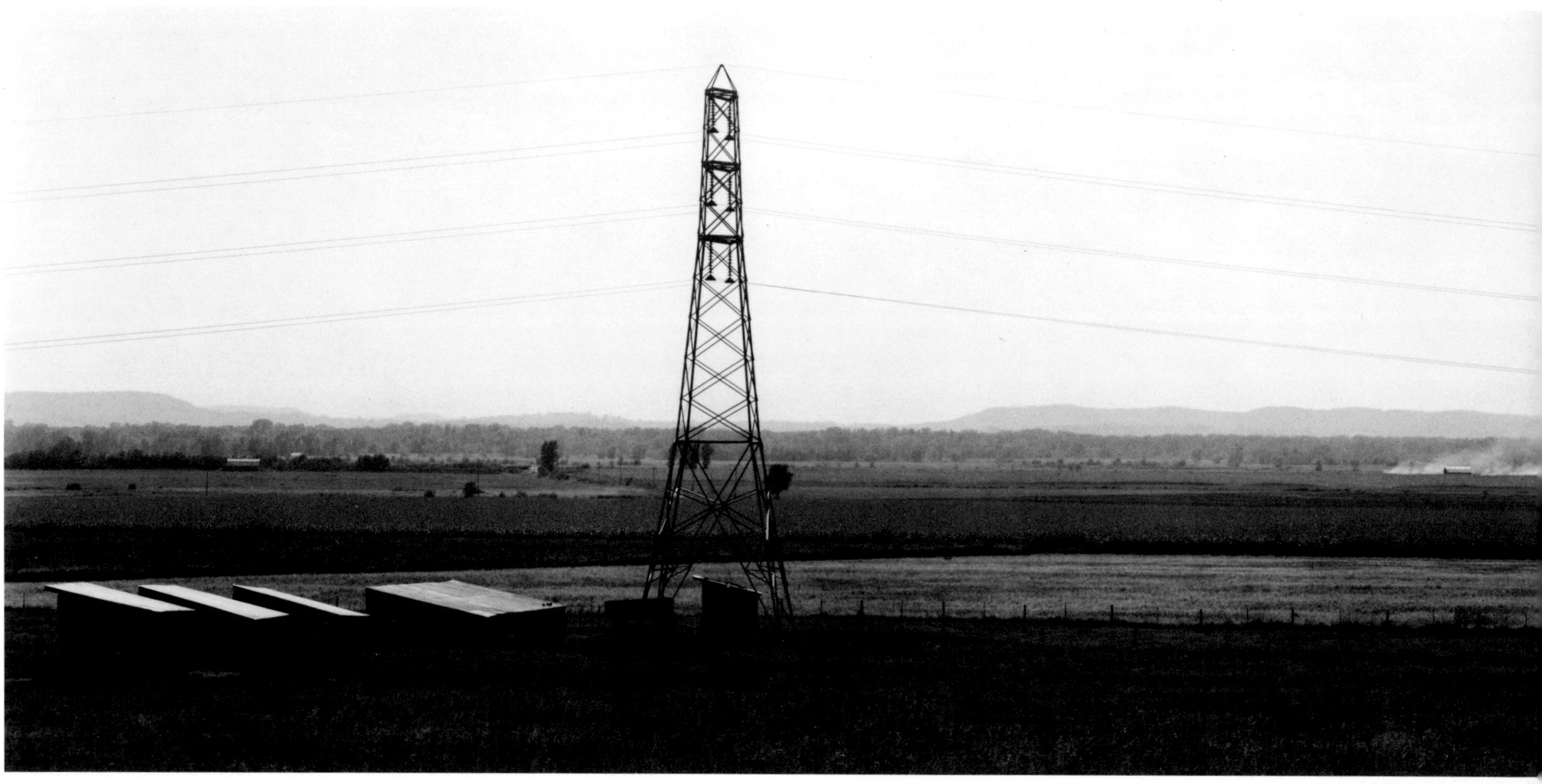

Sinsabaugh, Art
Midwest Landscape #78, 1963
silver gelatin print, 121 x 494mm.
Lent by the Art Institute of Chicago,
Restricted gift of the Joseph and Helen
Regenstein Foundation, 1963.750.

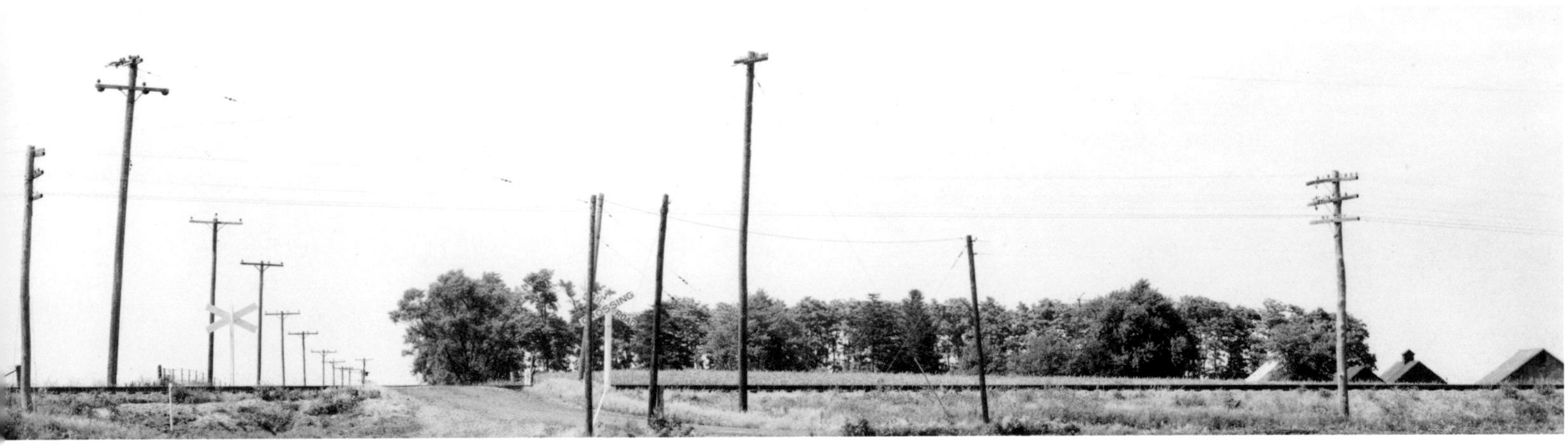

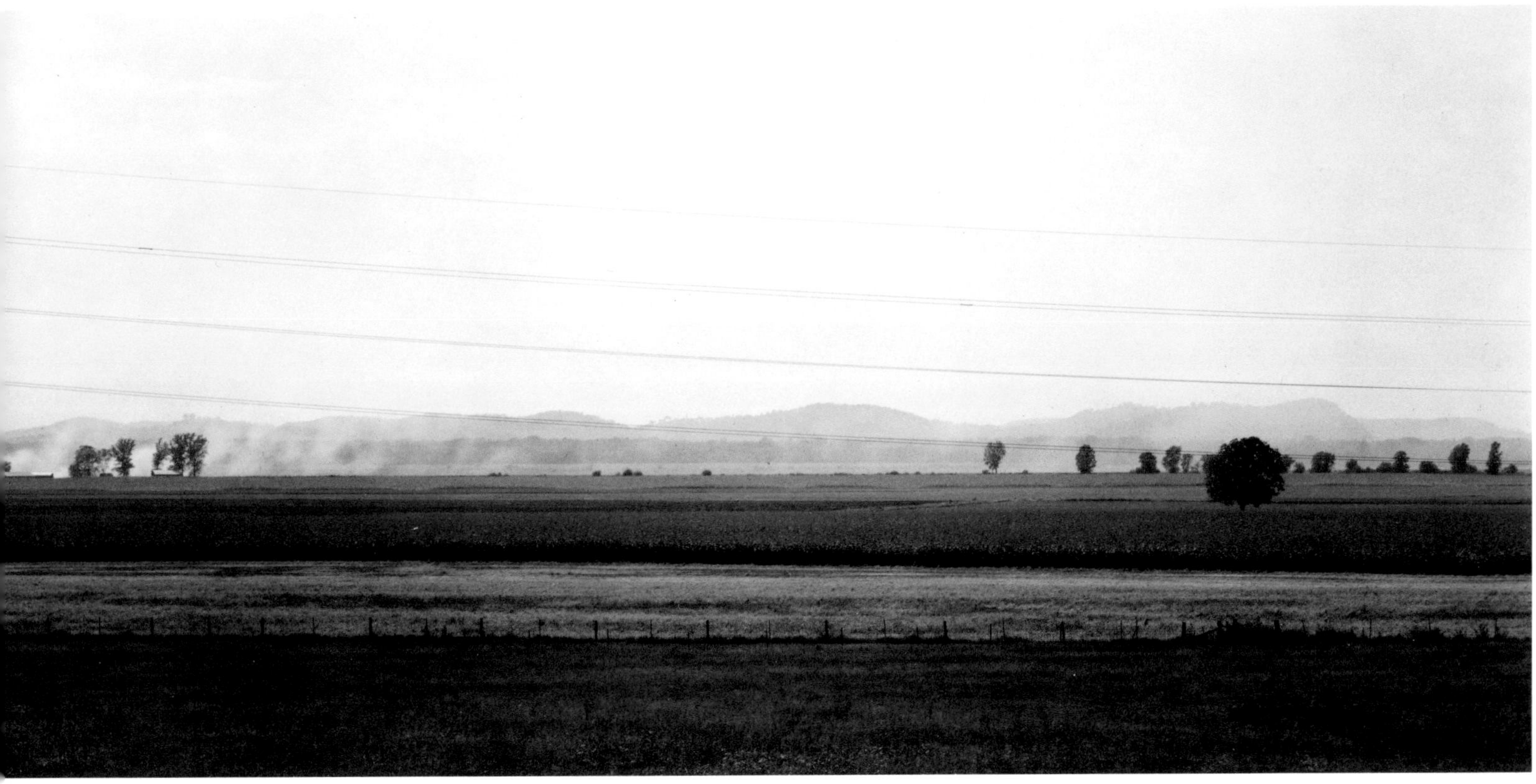

Midwest

Indiana: no blustering summit or coarse gorge;
No flora lurid as disaster-flares;
No great vacuities where tourists gape
Nor mountains hoarding their height like millionaires.
More delicate: the ten-foot knolls
Give flavor of hill to Indiana souls.

Topography is perfect, curio-size;
Deft as landscape in museum cases.
What is beautiful is friendly and underfoot,
Not flaunted like theater curtains in our faces.
No peak or jungle obscures the blue sky;
Our land rides smoothly in the softest eye.

Man is the prominent fauna of our state.
Elsewhere circus creatures stomp and leer
With heads like crags or clumps. But delirious nature
Once in a lucid interval sobering here
Left (repenting her extravagant plan)
Conspicuous on our fields the shadow of man.

JOHN F. NIMS

From Selected Poems by John Frederick Nims,
University of Chicago Press, 1982; Chicago, page 22.
Reprinted by permission.

Bill, Frank
Aerial View, McLean County, Illinois, 1930
silver gelatin print, 124 x 167mm.
Lent by the Bloomington, Illinois,
Daily Pantagraph.

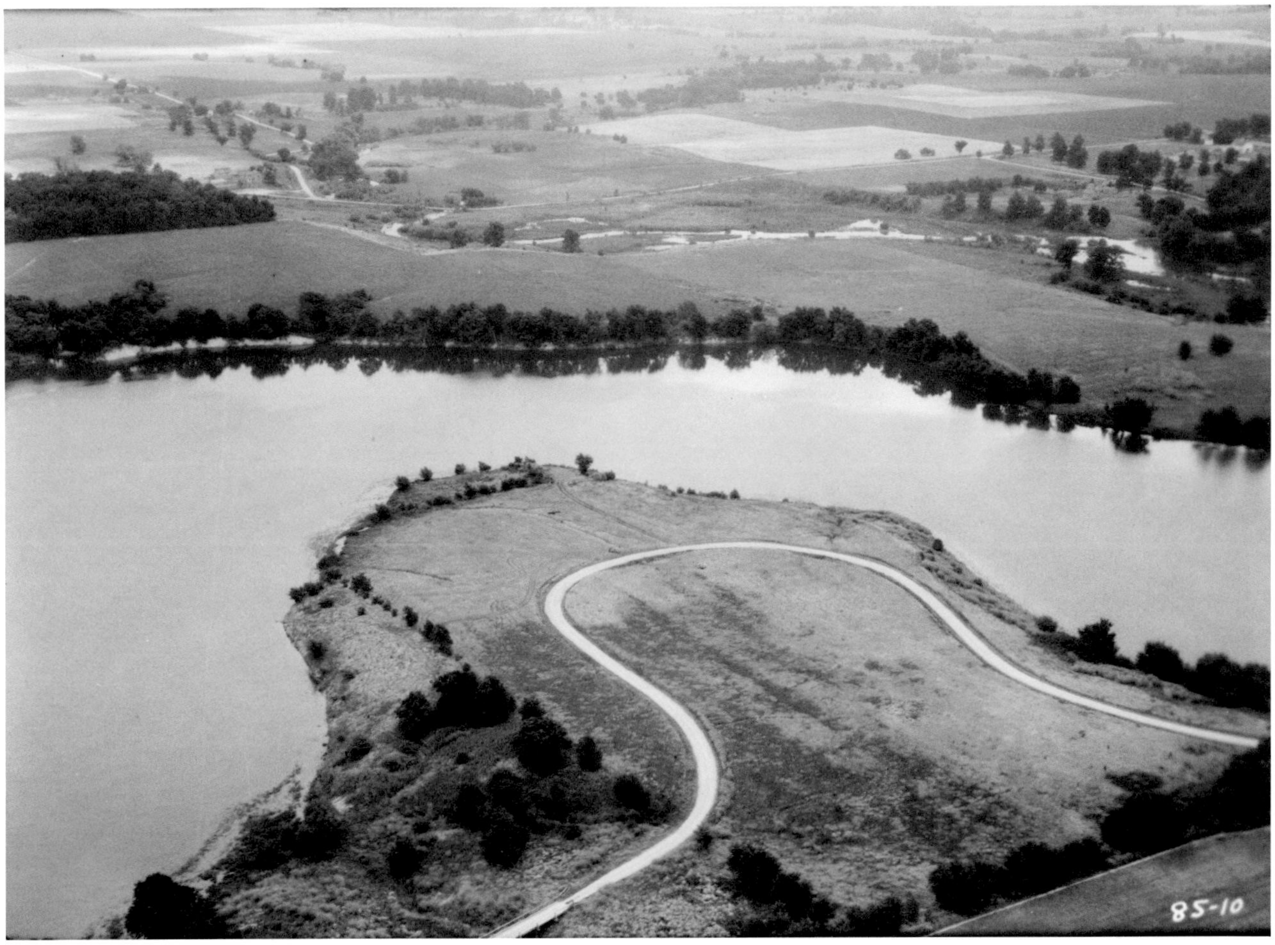

Rothstein, Arthur
Iowa, 1937
(LC34 29420)
silver gelatin print, 179 x 240mm.
From a negative in the collection
of the Prints and Photographs Division,
Library of Congress, Washington, D.C.
Lent by Open Lands Project of Chicago.

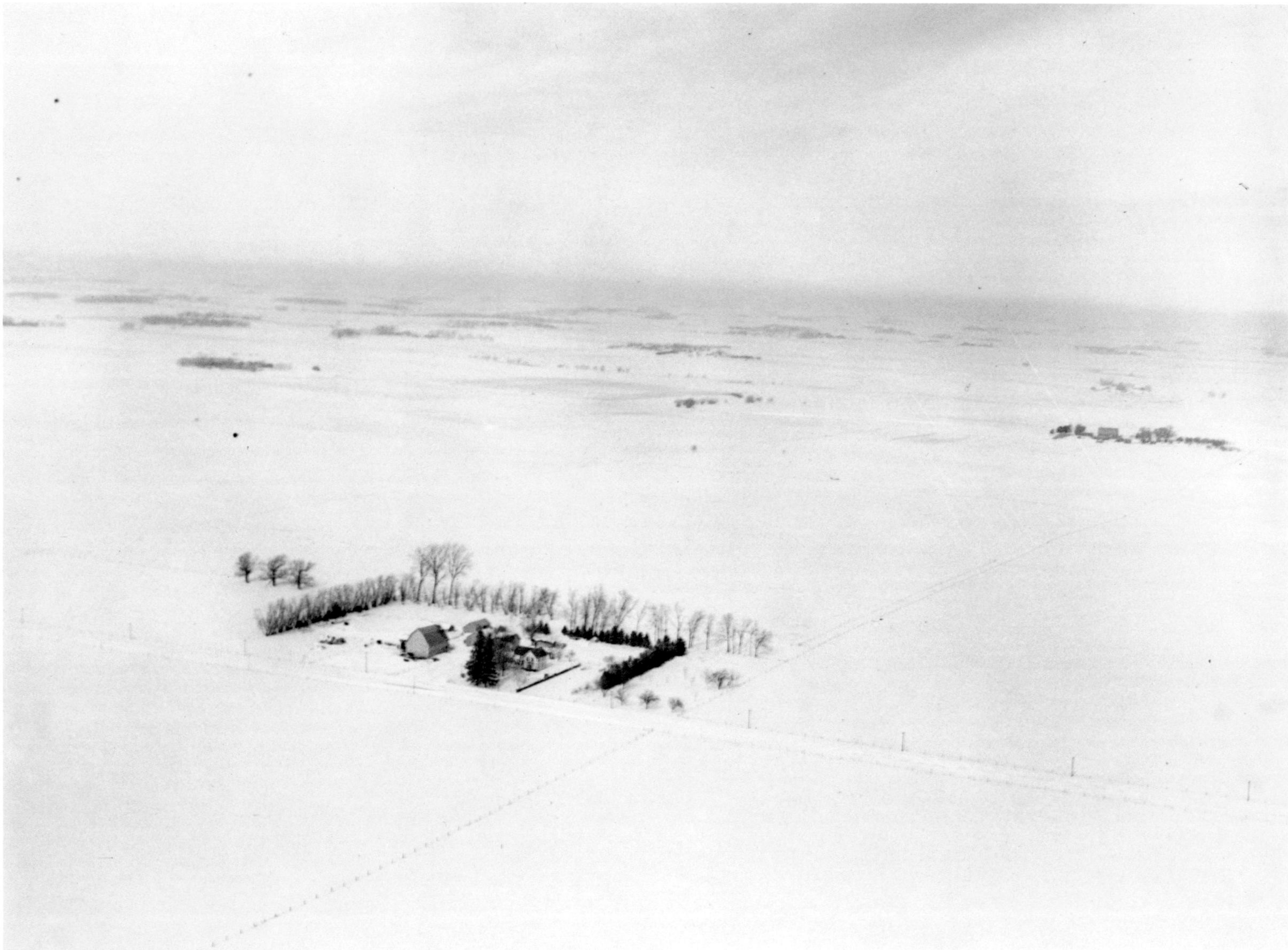

Morris, Wright
House in Winter, Near Lincoln, 1941
silver gelatin print, 192 x 241mm.
Lent by The Weston Gallery, Inc.,
Carmel, California.

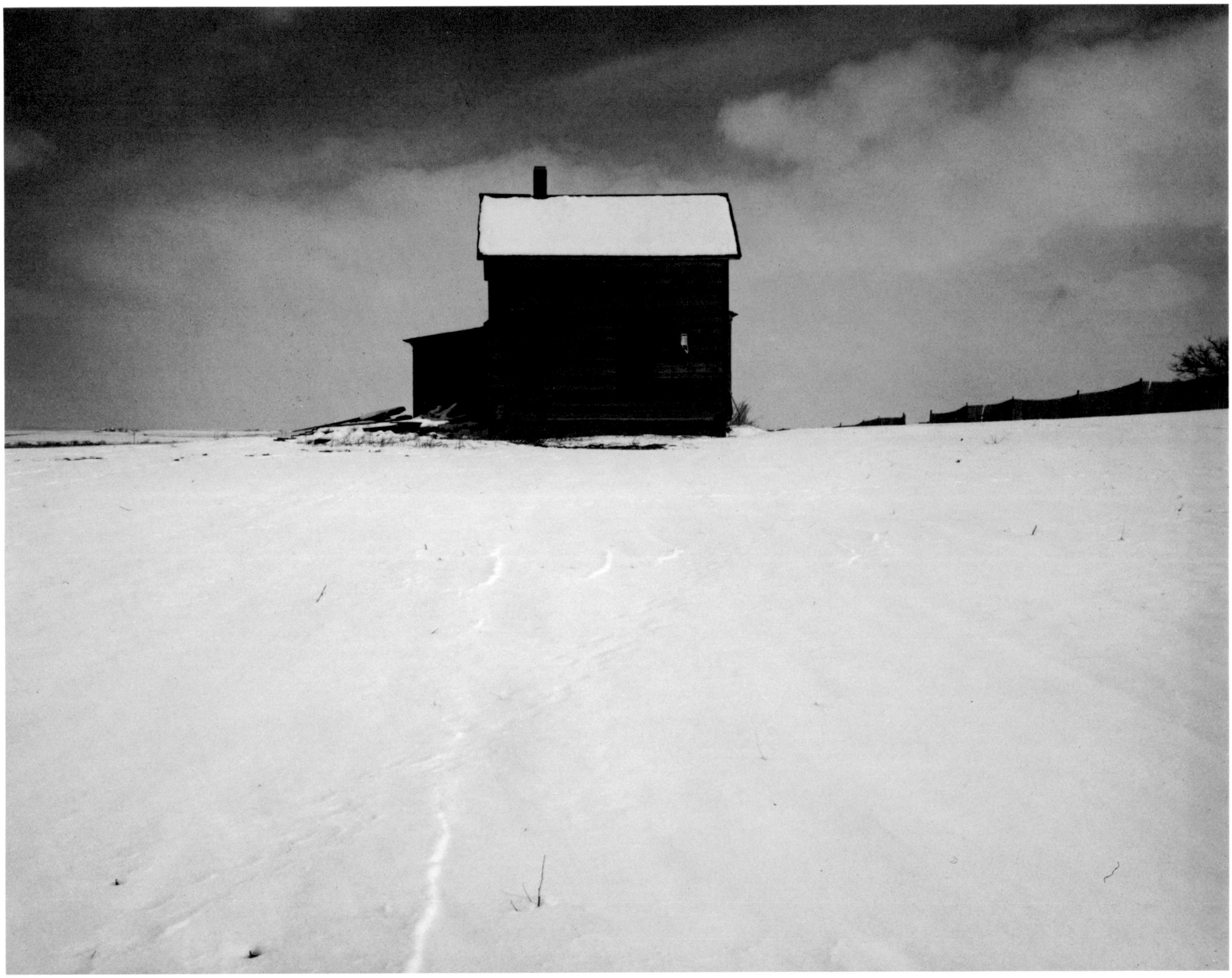

Neal Fox Studio, Thief River Falls, Minnesota
Combines on the Frank Keine Farm, Marshall County, c. 1960
silver gelatin print, 195 x 244mm.
Lent by the Minnesota Historical Society, St. Paul, Minnesota.

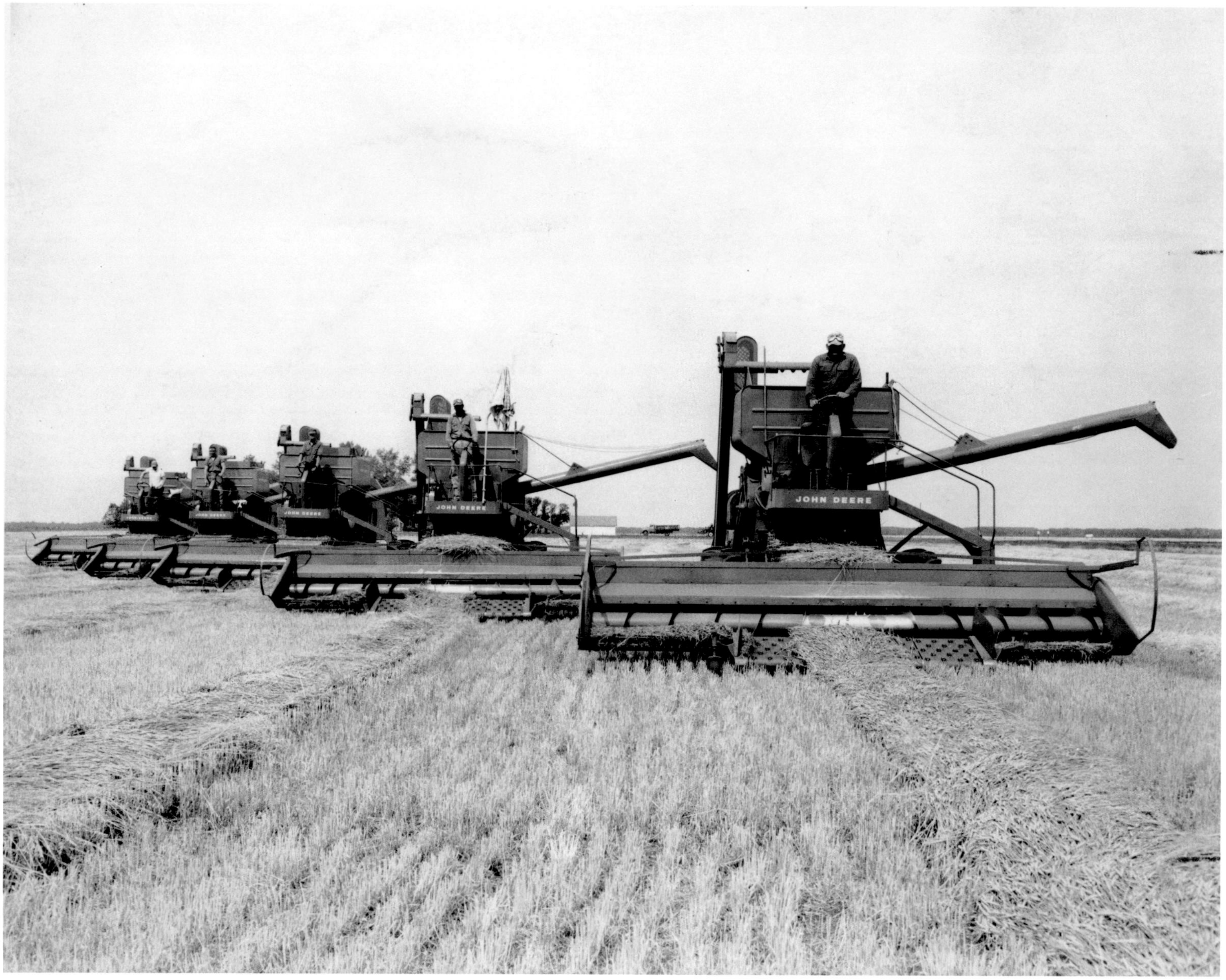

Culture of Corn

The great machines that mouse these fields
In May, between the long, dark showers—
How they do master and despise
The stick, the hoe that once were ours.

Even the coulter, tearing sod,
Even the horses, our huge slaves—
The red machines remember nothing.
Man and beast are in their graves,

And only metal that moves itself
Goes back and forth here, biting in.
Yet truth to say, the softened fields,
Supine, are willing that it win.

They lie there, those great breeding queens,
Brown at the breast and cool of womb,
And wait for seed; nor ever sigh
Because no two feet, four feet come.

MARK VAN DOREN

Vanderbilt, Paul
Near Coon Valley, Wisconsin, 1962
silver gelatin print, 215 x 300mm.
Lent by the Art Institute of Chicago,
Gift of the photographer and the State
Historical Society of Wisconsin, 1965.905.

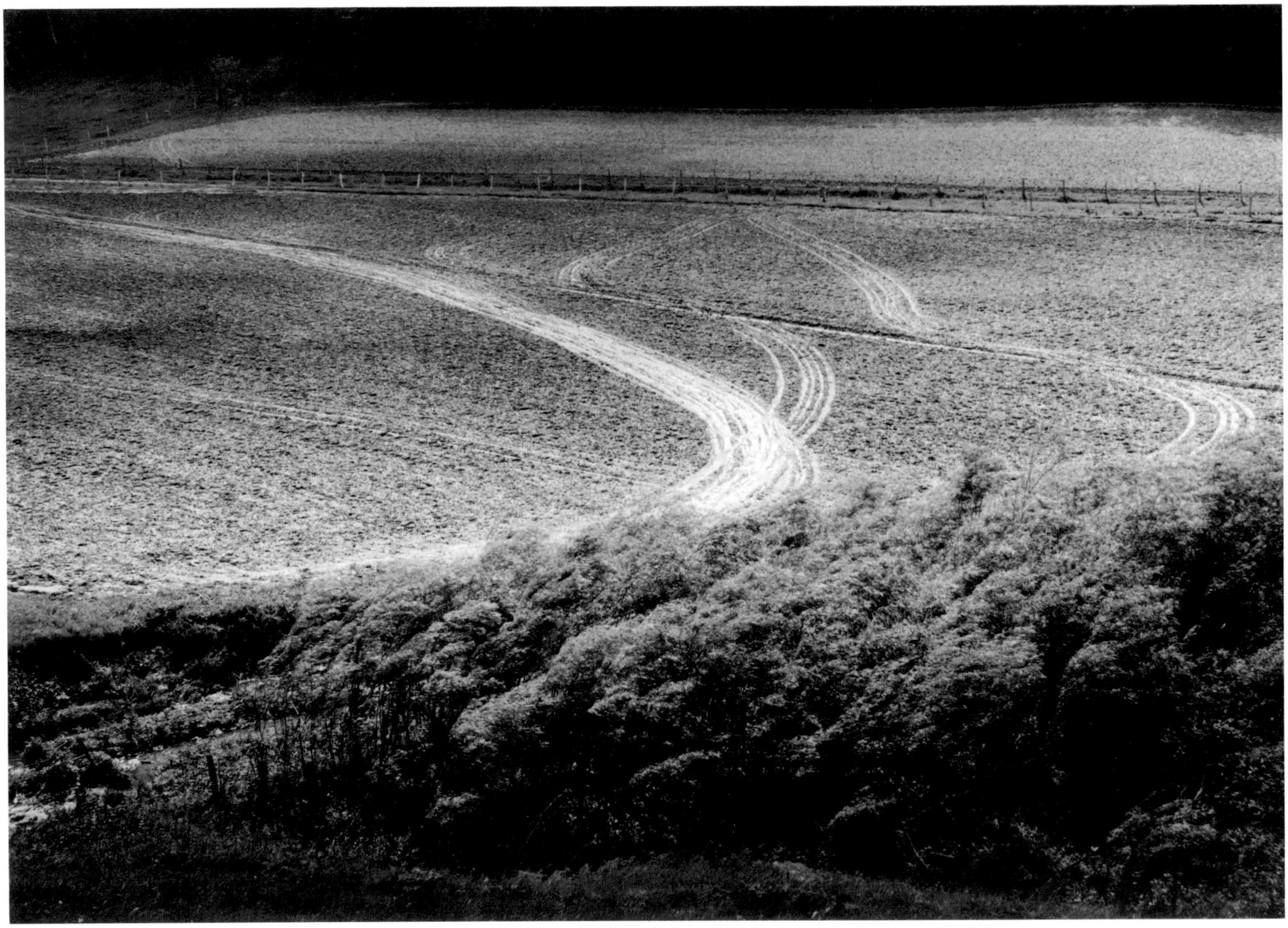

Vanderbilt, Paul
Field Road Near
Black Earth, Wisconsin, 1962
silver gelatin print, 204 x 333mm.
Lent by the Art Institute of Chicago,
Gift of the photographer and the State
Historical Society of Wisconsin, 1965.904.

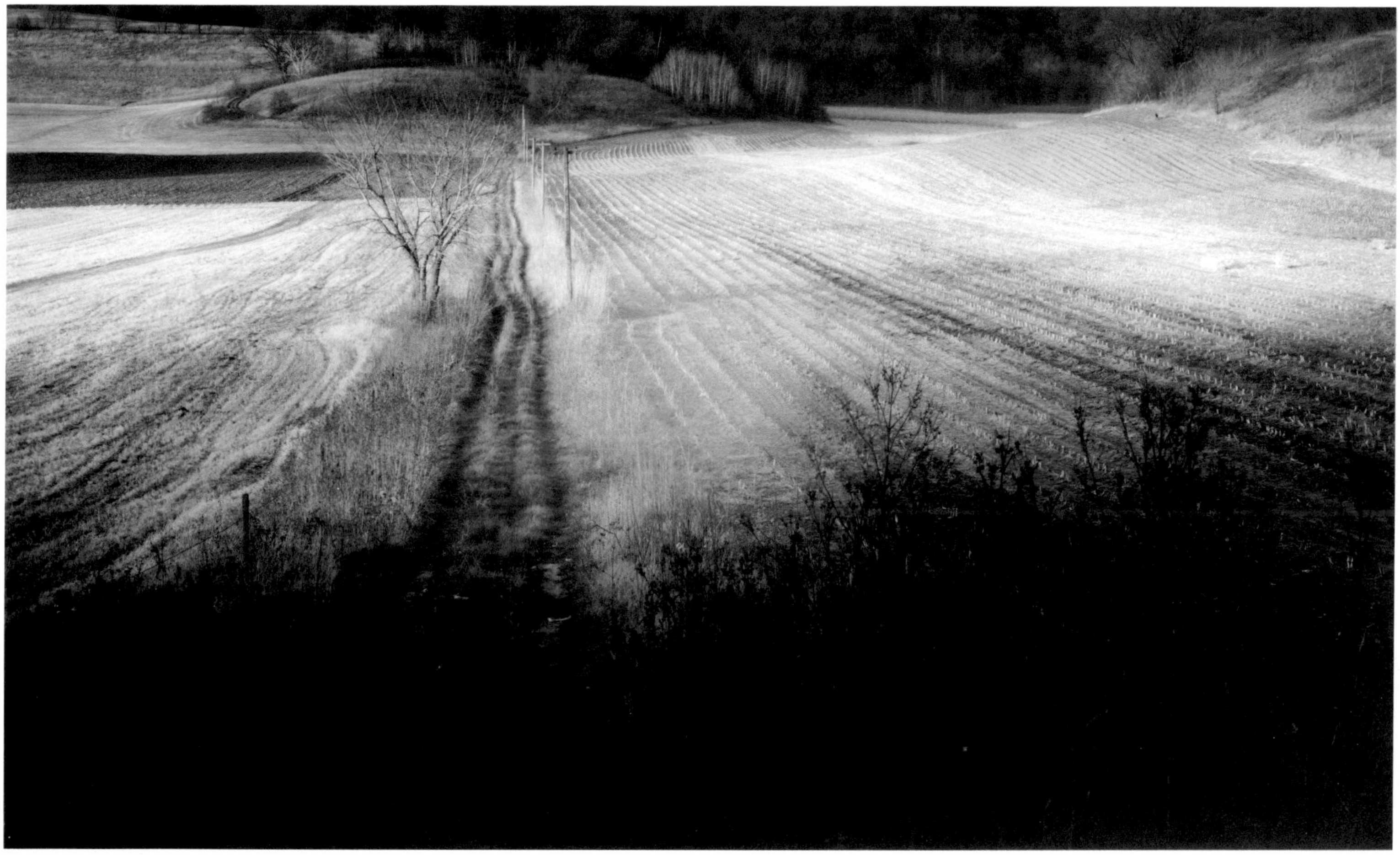

Enyeart, James

Riley County, No. 3, c. 1970
silver gelatin print, 254 x 327 mm.
Lent by the Spencer Museum of Art,
The University of Kansas, Lawrence, Kansas.

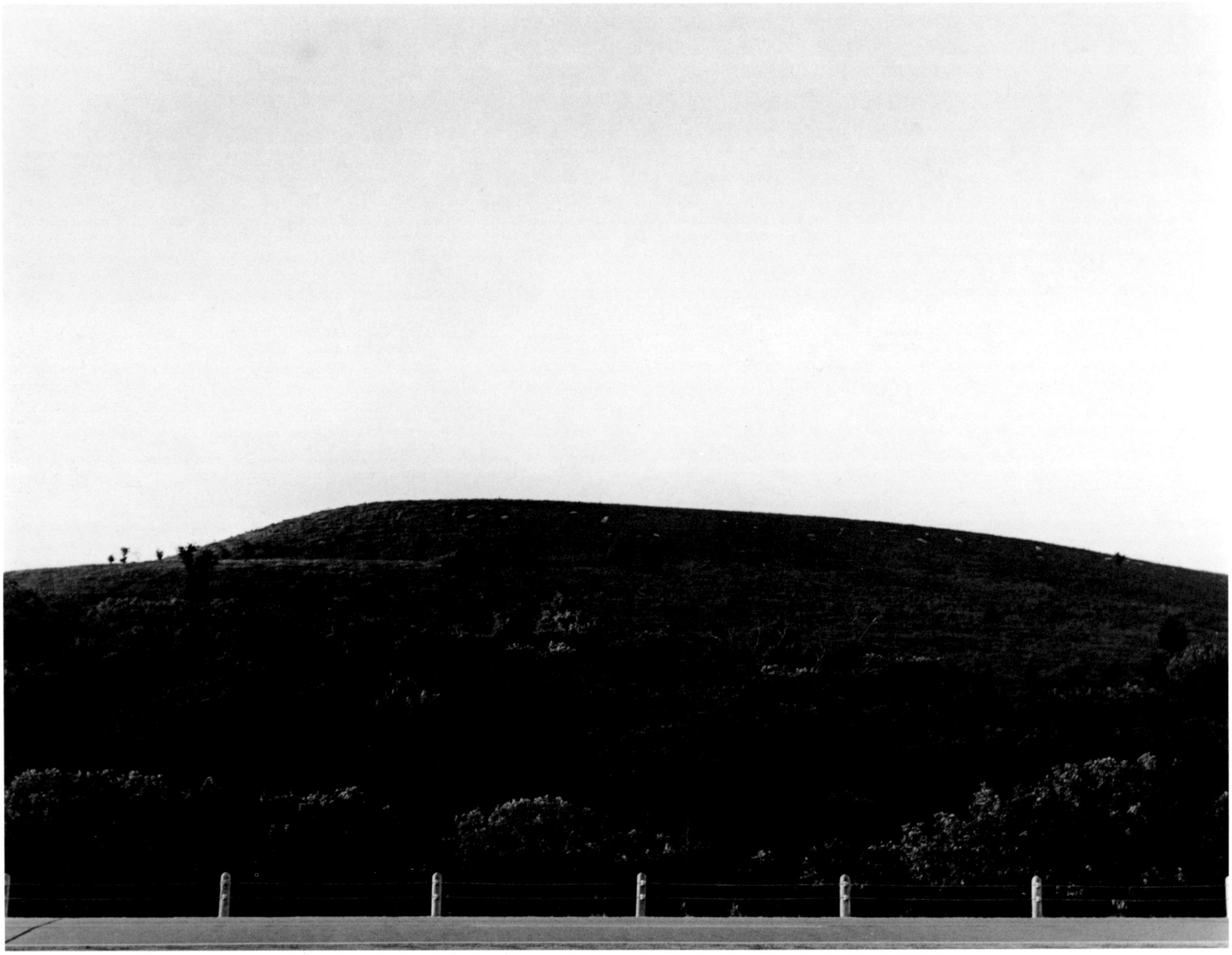

Boersma, Jay
Northern Indiana, 1973-74
silver gelatin print, 203 x 253mm.
Lent by the photographer.

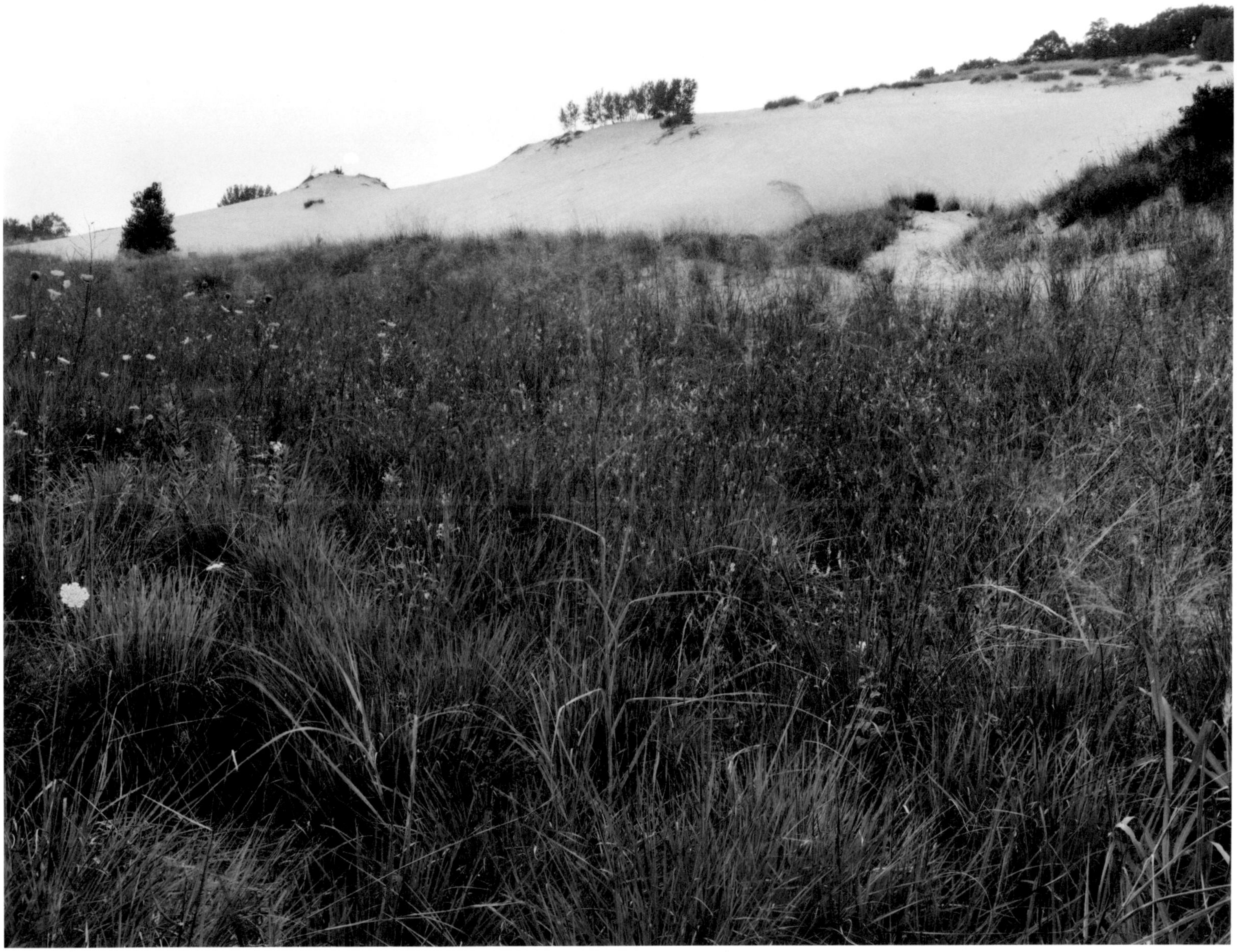

To make a prairie it takes a clover and one bee,
One clover, and a bee,
And revery.
The revery alone will do,
If bees are few.

By EMILY DICKINSON
Complete Poems, by Emily Dickinson. Edited by Thomas A. Johnson. First Edition. Little, Brown, 1965. Boston. Page 710.

McFarland, Lawrence
Wheatfield, 1976
silver gelatin print, 265 x 430mm.
Lent by the photographer.

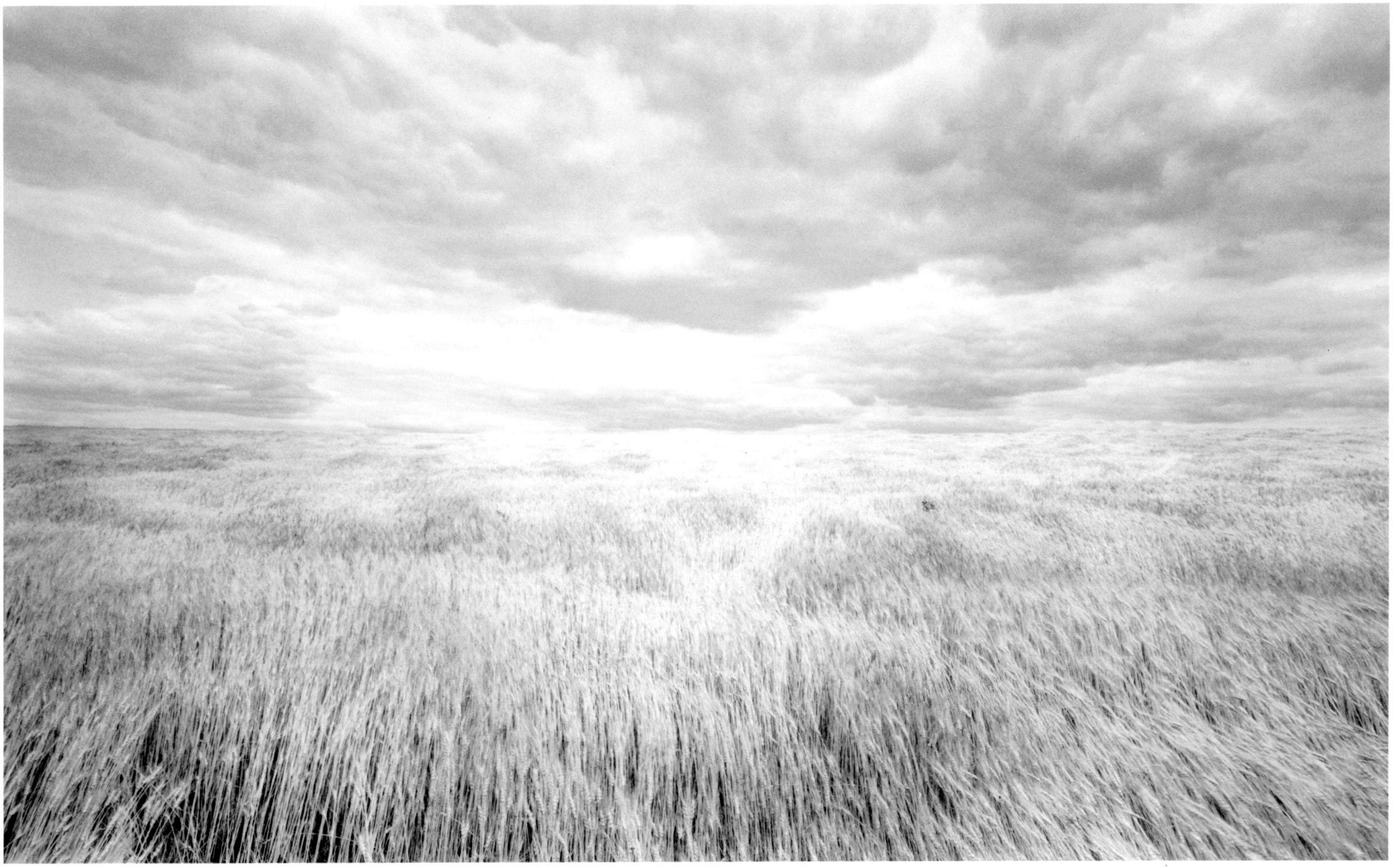

Woods, Lucia
Ivar's Pond, 1972
silver gelatin print, 202 x 305mm.
Lent by The Art Institute of Chicago,
Mary and Leigh Block Fund for Acquisitions,
1975.579.

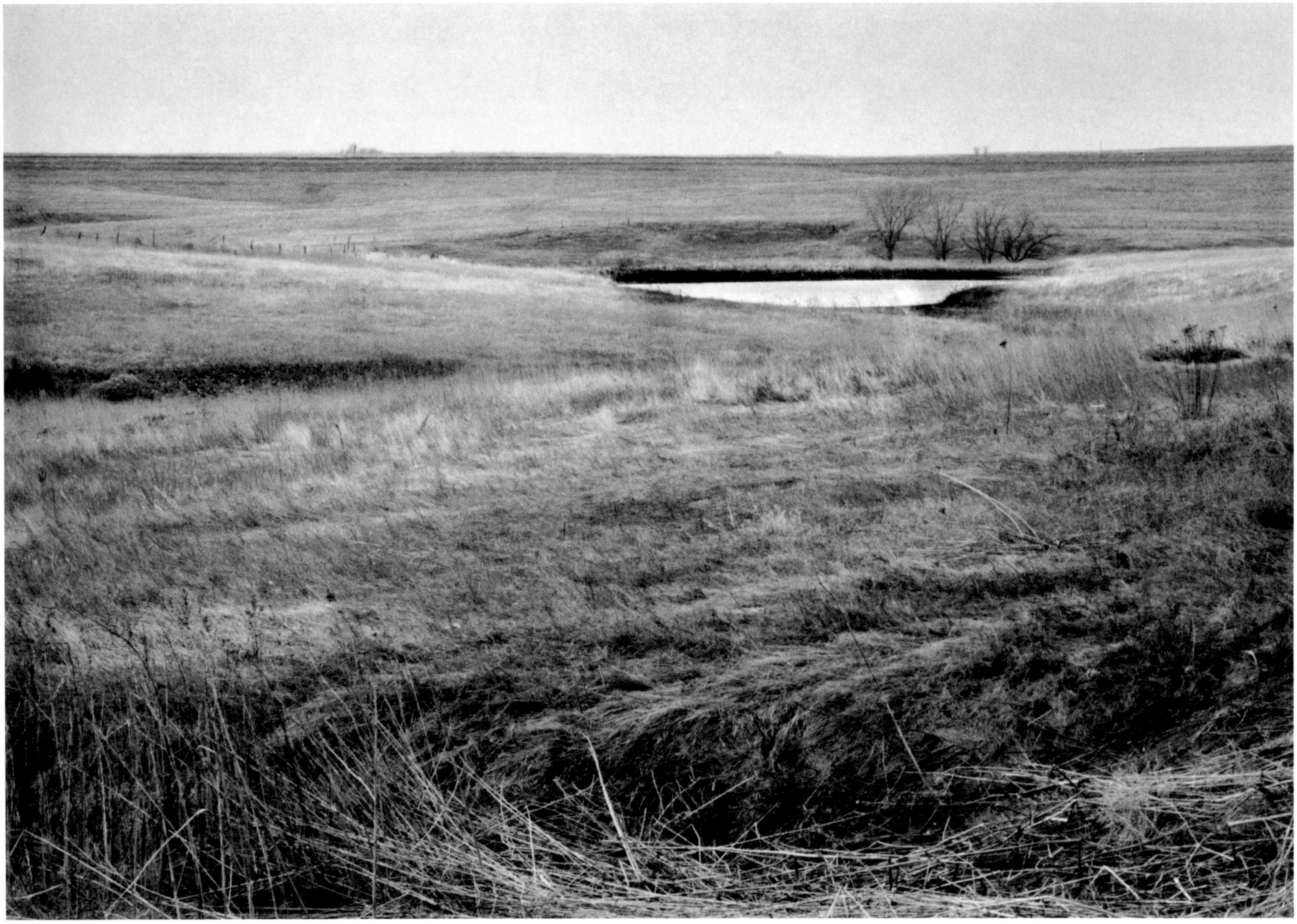

Adams, Robert
Missouri River, Clay County, S.D., 1977
silver gelatin print, 231 x 297mm.
Lent by The Art Institute of Chicago
Restricted gift of Louise Lutz, 1982.138.

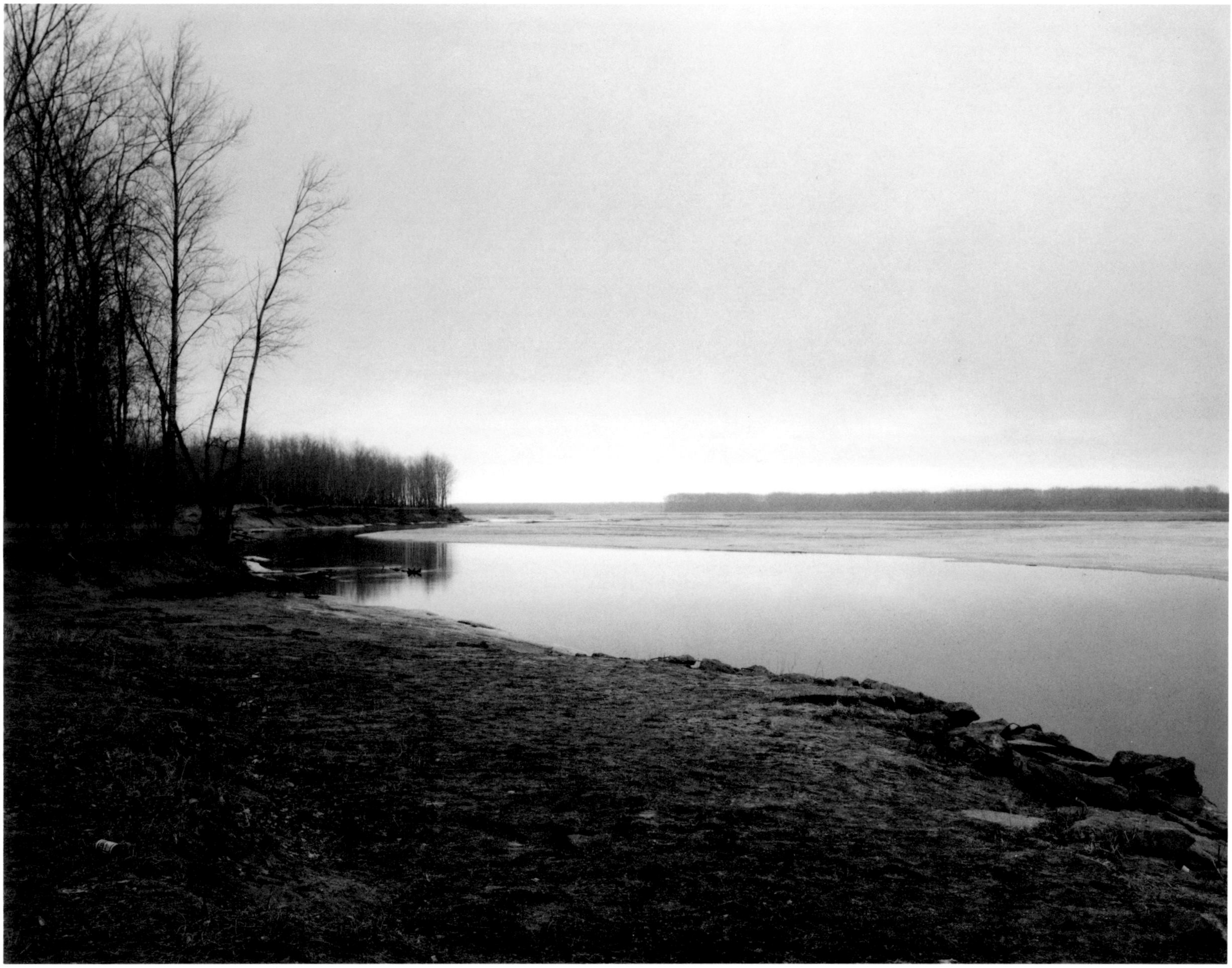

Johnson, Michael
Watercourse, 1976
silver gelatin print, 215 x 313mm.
On loan to the Art Institute of
Chicago from Jack and Roberta Jaffe.

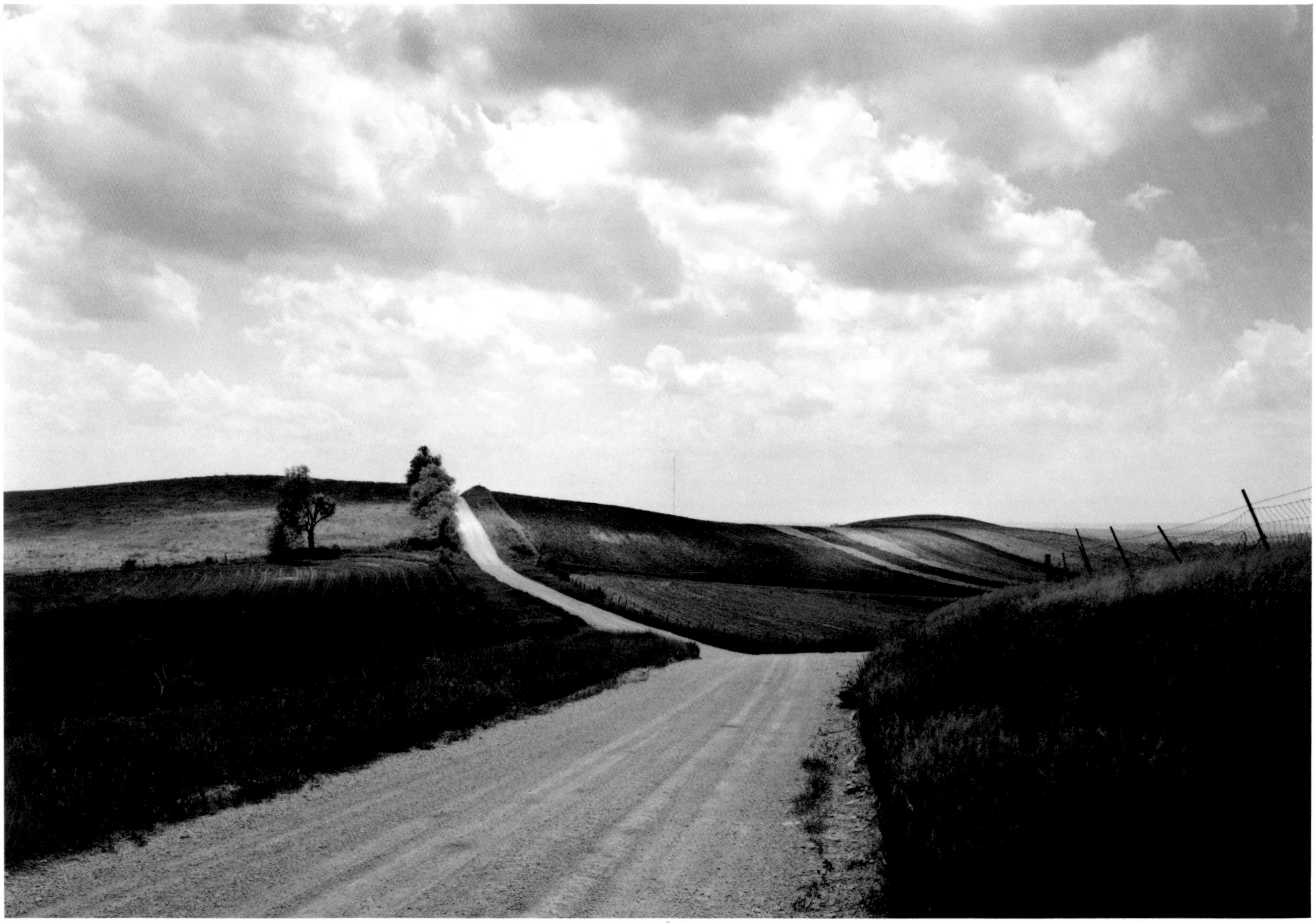

McFarland, Lawrence
Near Linsborg, Kansas, 1976
silver gelatin print, 265 x 430mm.
Lent by the photographer.

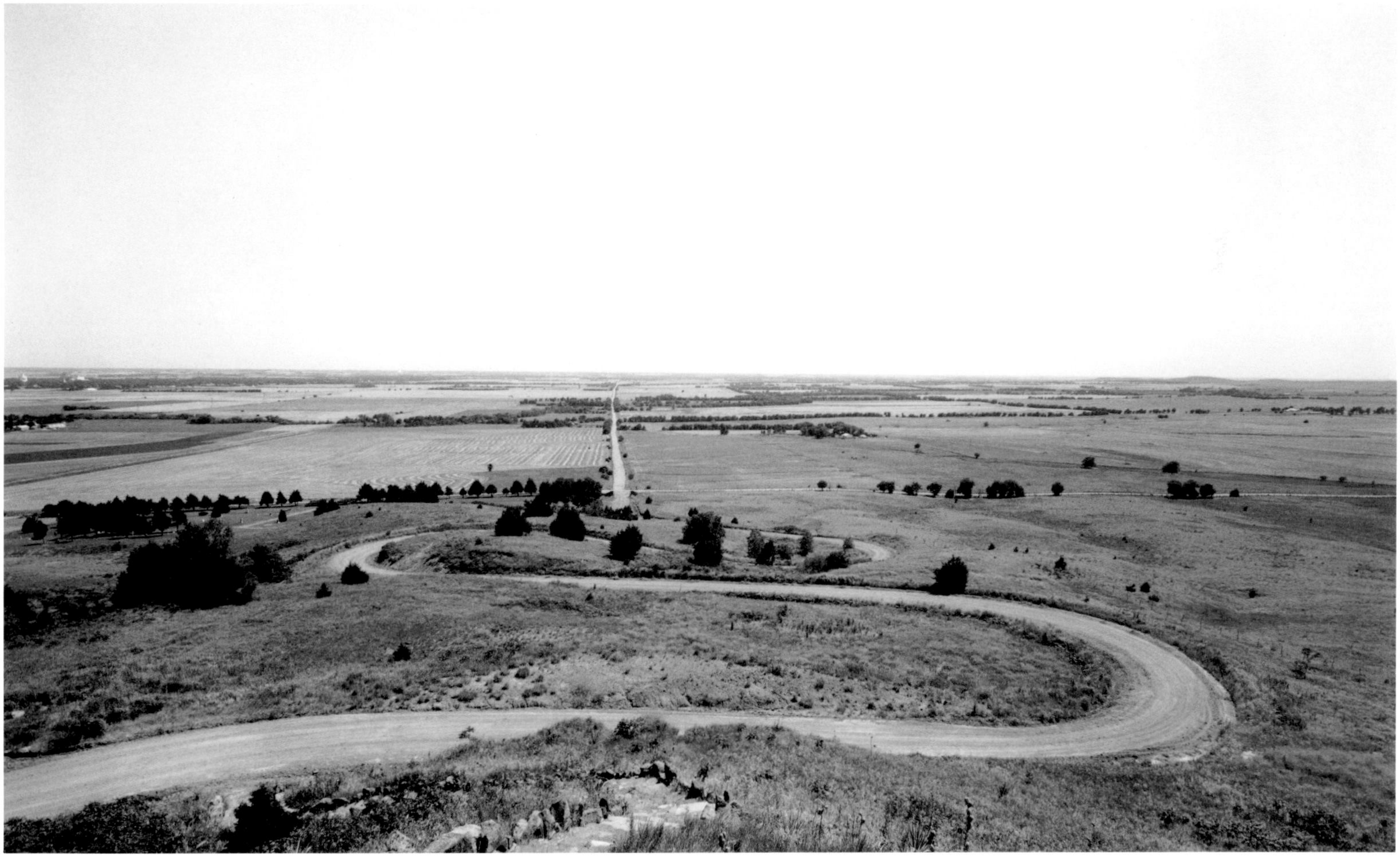

Deschamps, Francois
Landscape with Red Tree, 1979
color photograph, C-print, 203 x 305mm.
Lent by the photographer.

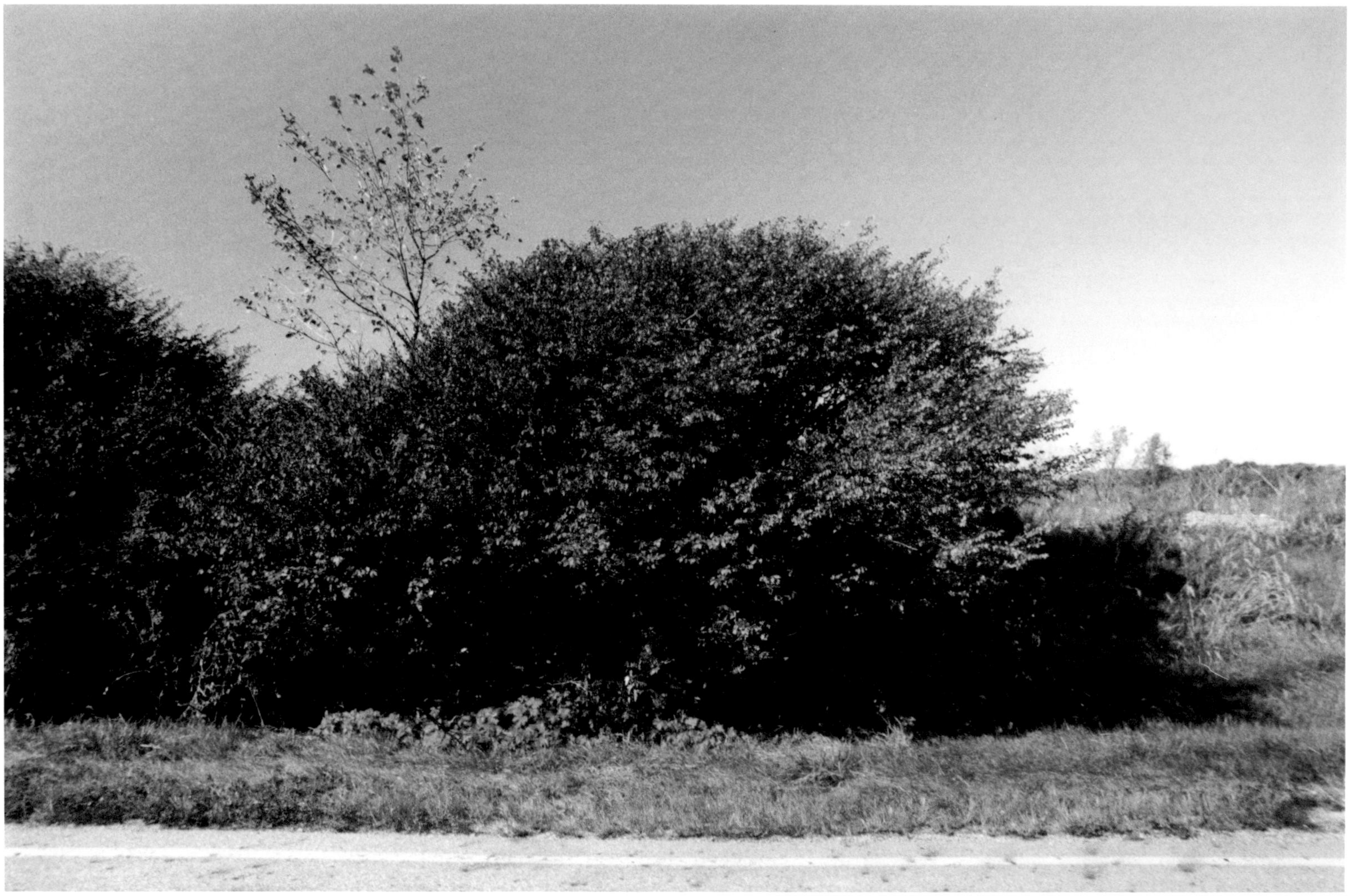

Schwarm, Larry
Cornfield near Colby, Kansas, c. 1975
color photograph, C-print, 217 x 319mm.
Lent by the photographer.

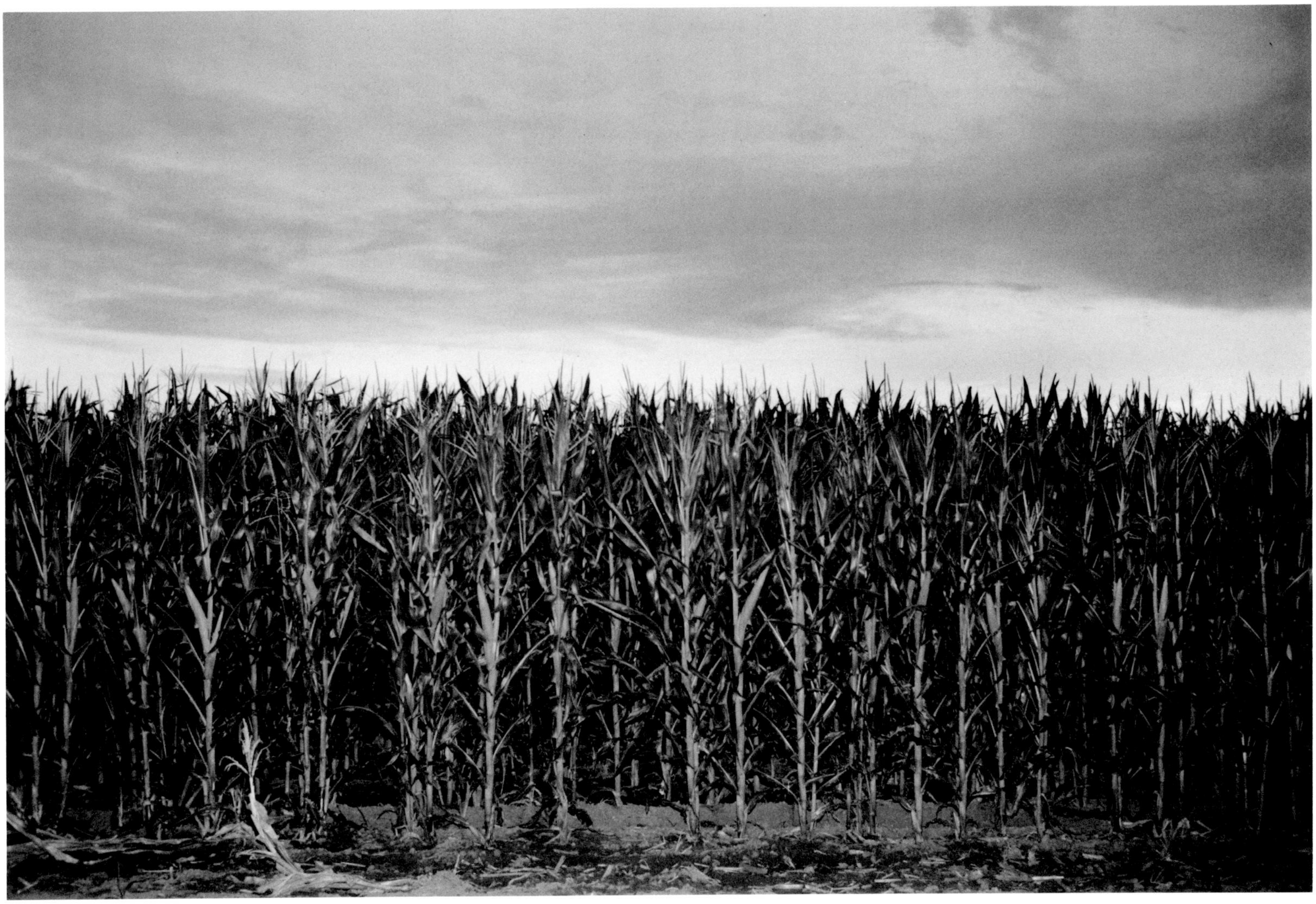

Gohlke, Frank
Farm Yard Near Houston, Minnesota, 1977
silver gelatin print, 279 x 347mm.
Lent by the photographer.

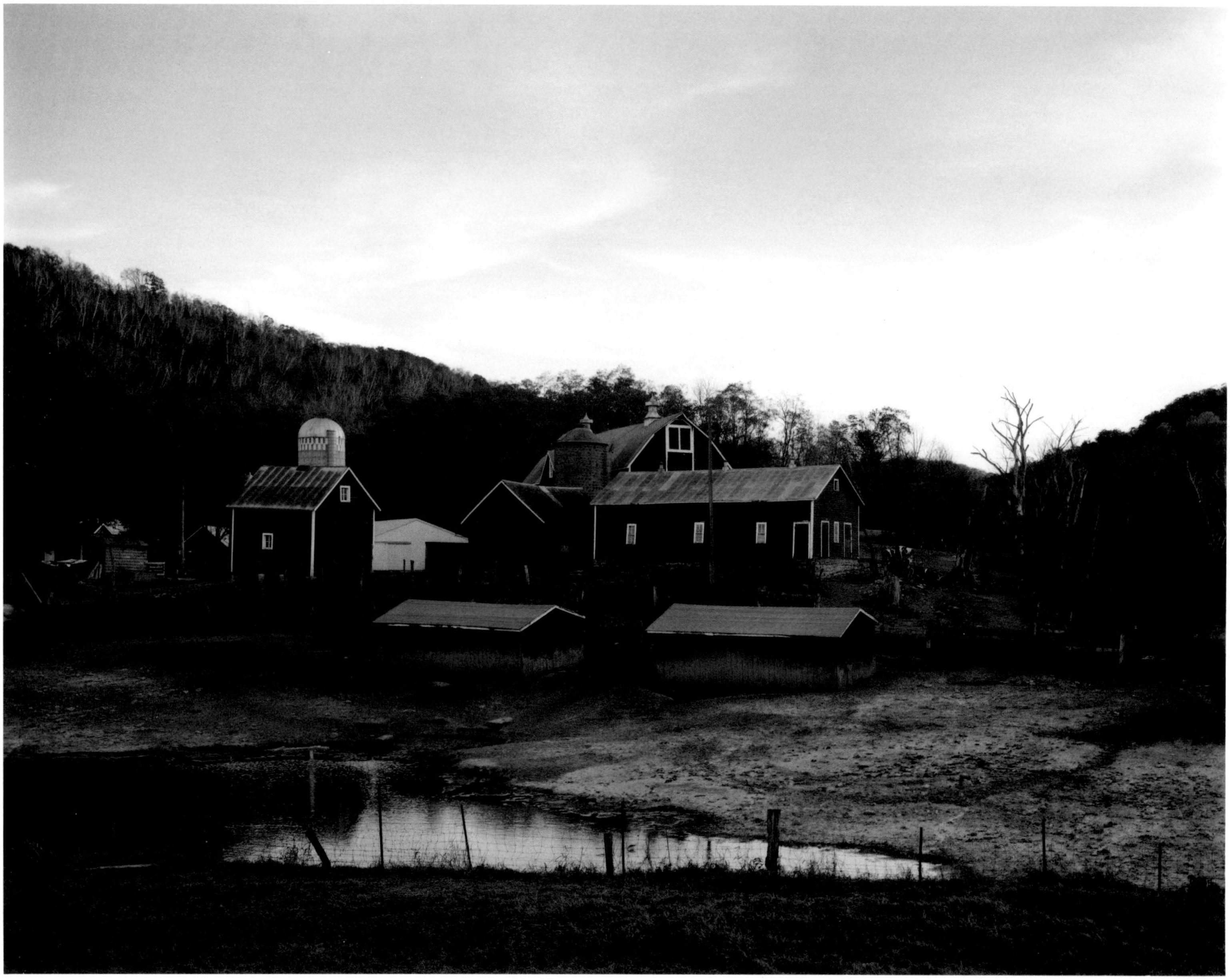

Cialdella, Gary A.
Landscape, Small Trees and Cornfield Near Berrien Springs, Michigan, 1981
silver gelatin print, 206 x 455mm.
Lent by the photographer.

Iversen, Earl
Flint Hills South of Emporia, Cattle Pens Area, Interstate 35, 1979
silver gelatin print, 218 x 328mm.
Lent by the photographer.

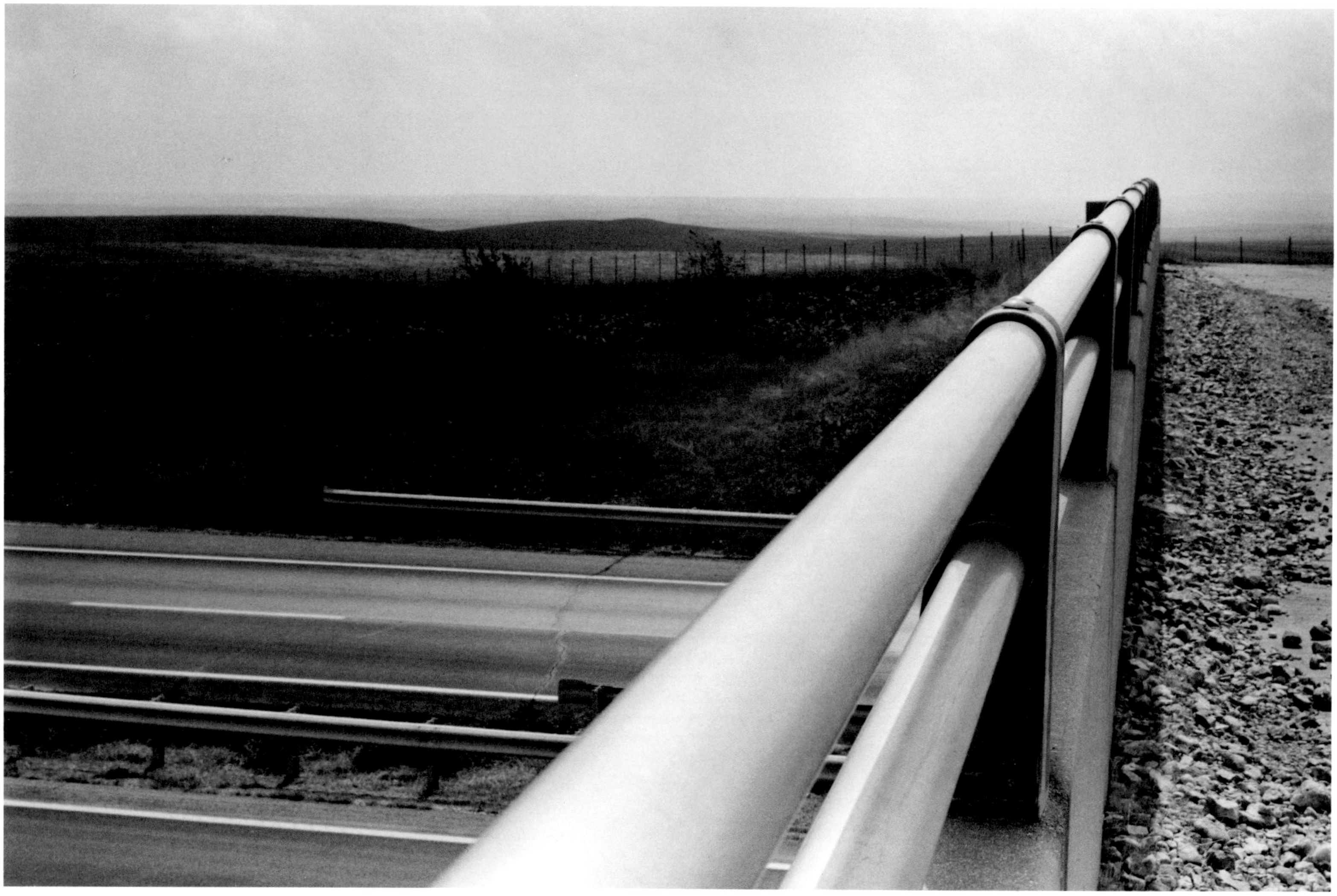

Davis, Keith F.
Field, Weston, Missouri, spring 1982
silver gelatin print, 194 x 243mm.
Lent by the photographer.

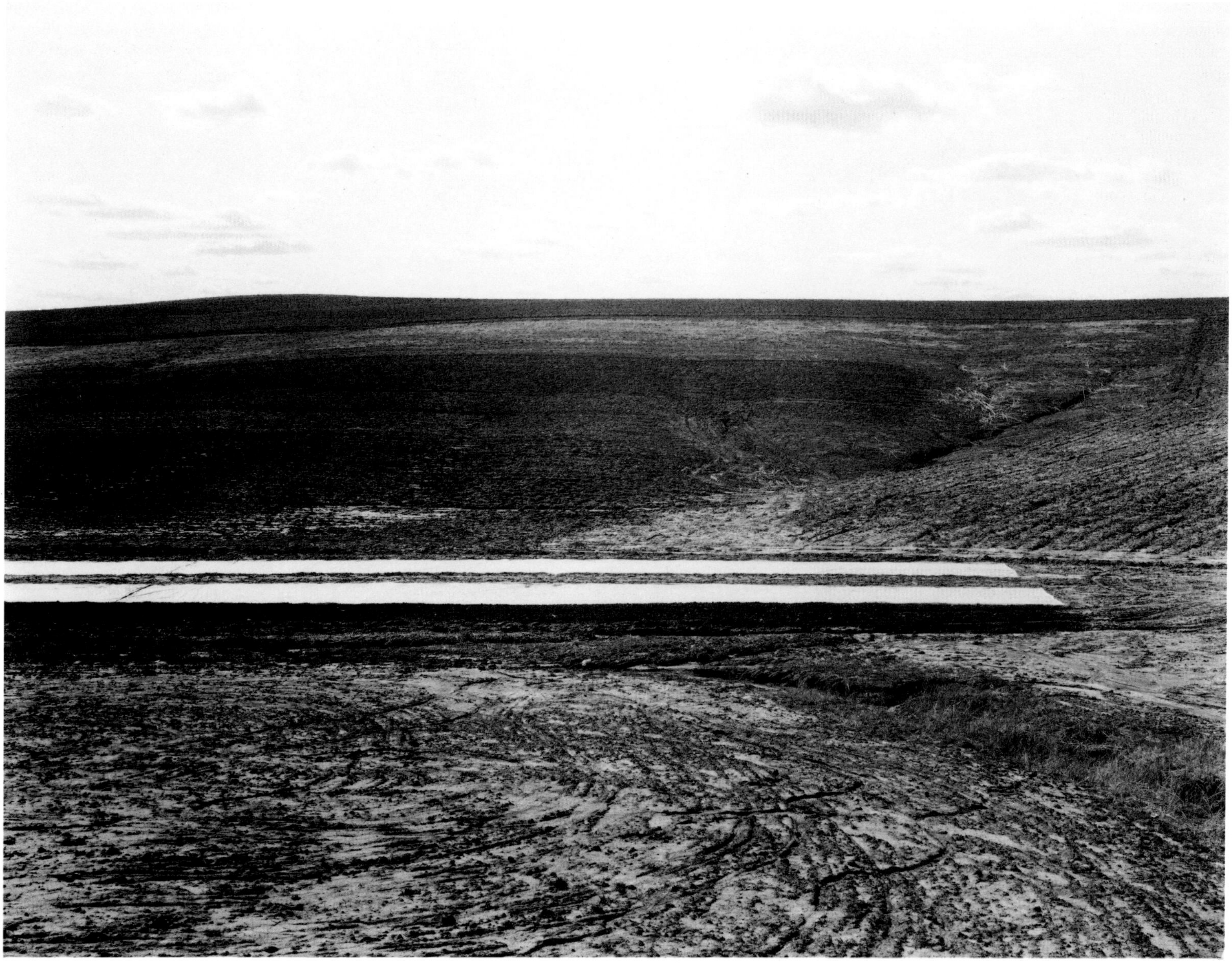

Morris, Wright
Abandoned Farm,
Western Nebraska, 1941
silver gelatin print, 192 x 241mm.
Lent by The Weston Gallery, Inc.,
Carmel, California.

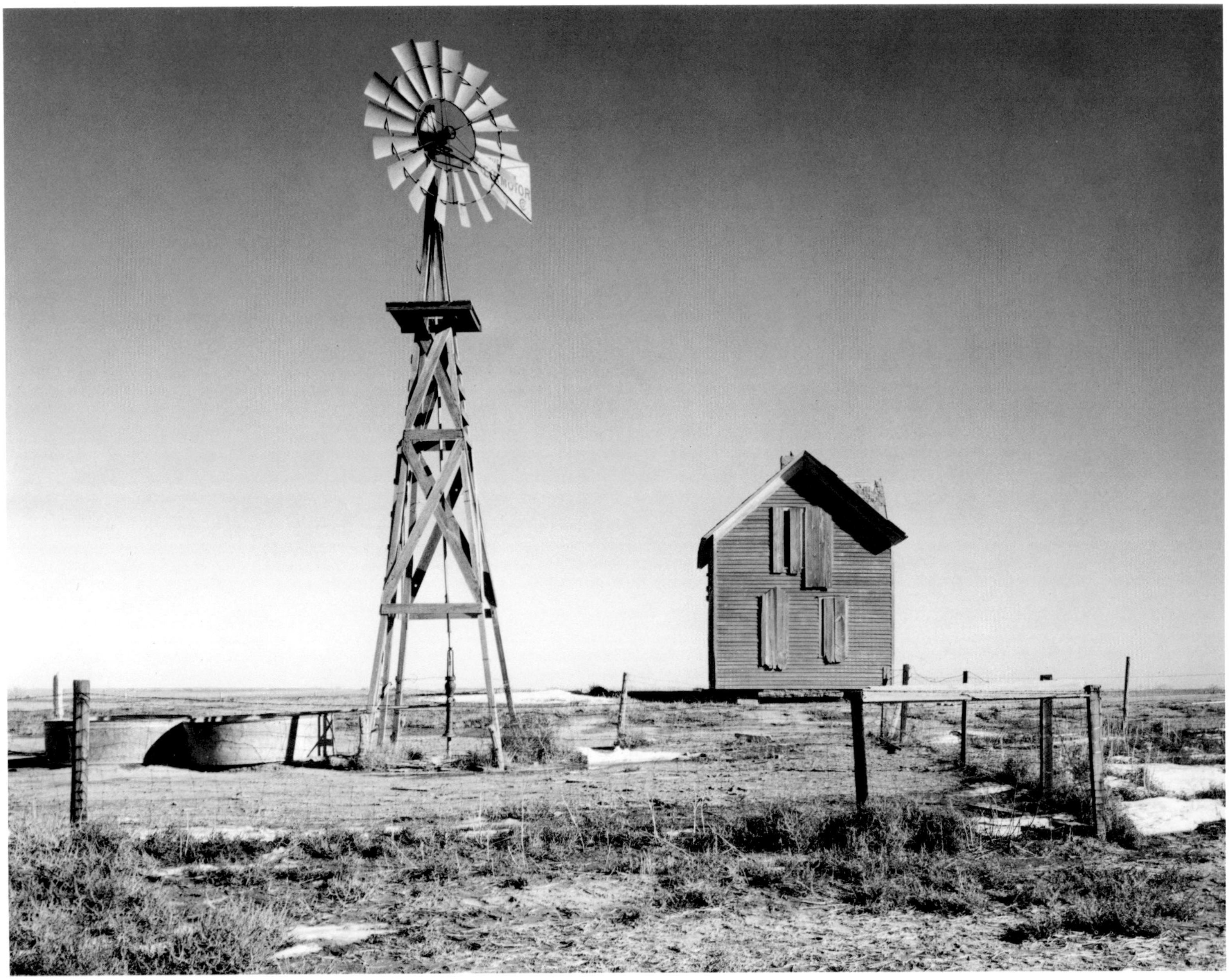

Ferguson, Larry
Polled Herefords,
Near Niobrara, Nebraska, 1981
chlorobromide silver print, 215 x 305mm.
Lent by the photographer.

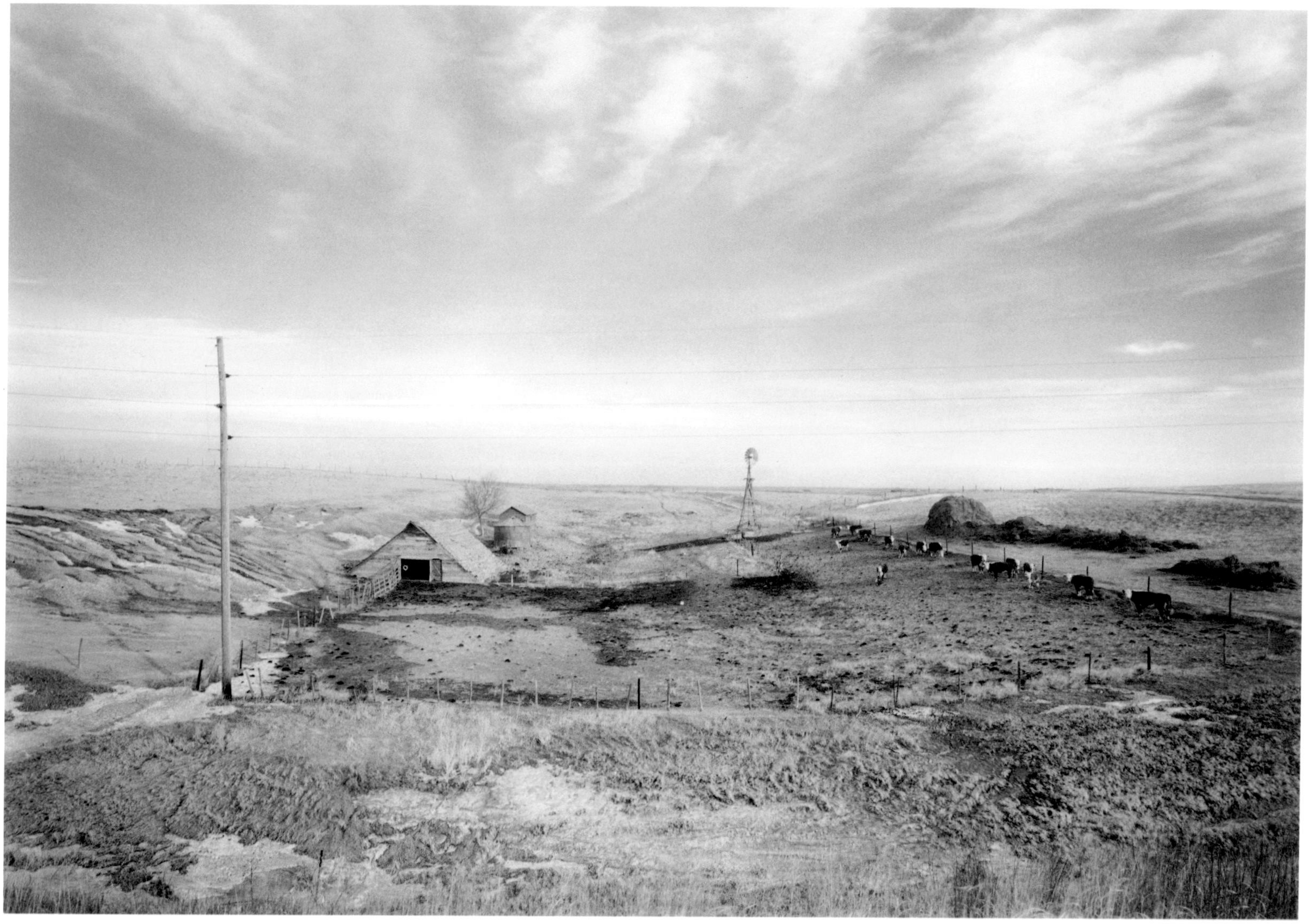

Plasko, Nancy Sparrow
Restored Prairie, Big Stone Wildlife Refuge, November 1980
silver gelatin print, 243 x 305mm.
Lent by the photographer.

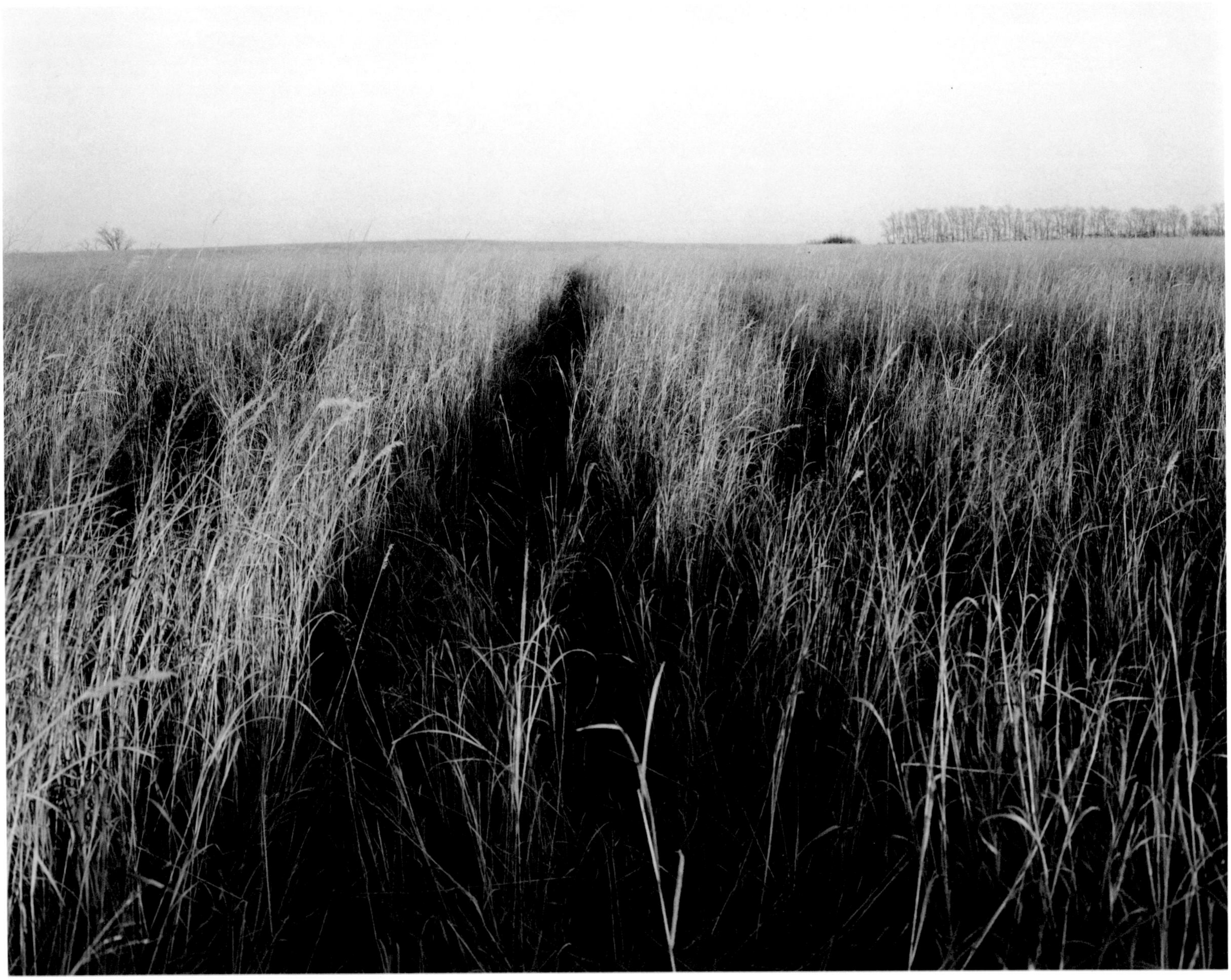

Lazar, Arthur
Ohio, 1978
platinum print, 120 x 170mm.
Lent by the photographer.

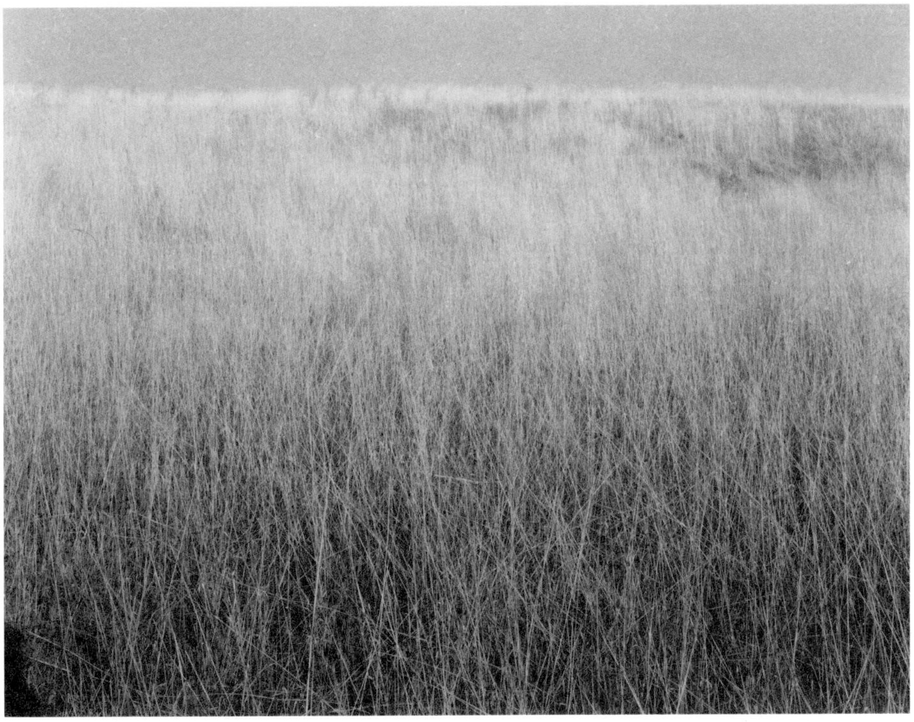

Plowden, David
Nuclear Generating Station,
Sillman Valley, Illinois, 1981
silver gelatin print, 241 x 325mm.
Lent by the photographer.

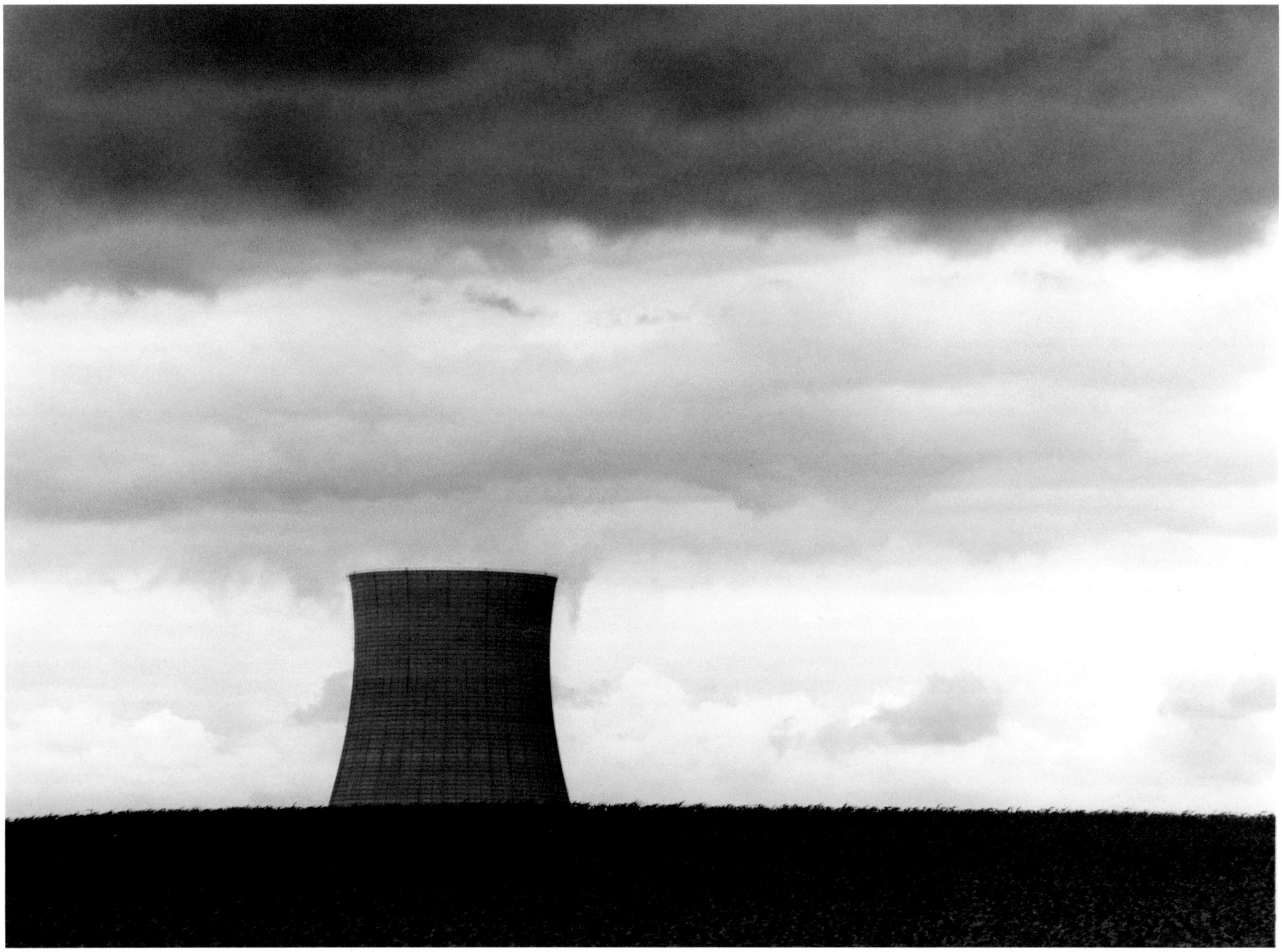

Plowden, David
Near Peotone, Illinois, 1981
silver gelatin print, 259 x 308mm.
Lent by the photographer.

Arndt, Tom
Bismarck, North Dakota, 1981
silver gelatin print, 316 x 473mm.
Lent by Henryka Frajlich-Manès.

Cheek, Vernon
Indiana Landscape, 1982
color photograph, C-print, 130 x 166mm.
Lent by the photographer.

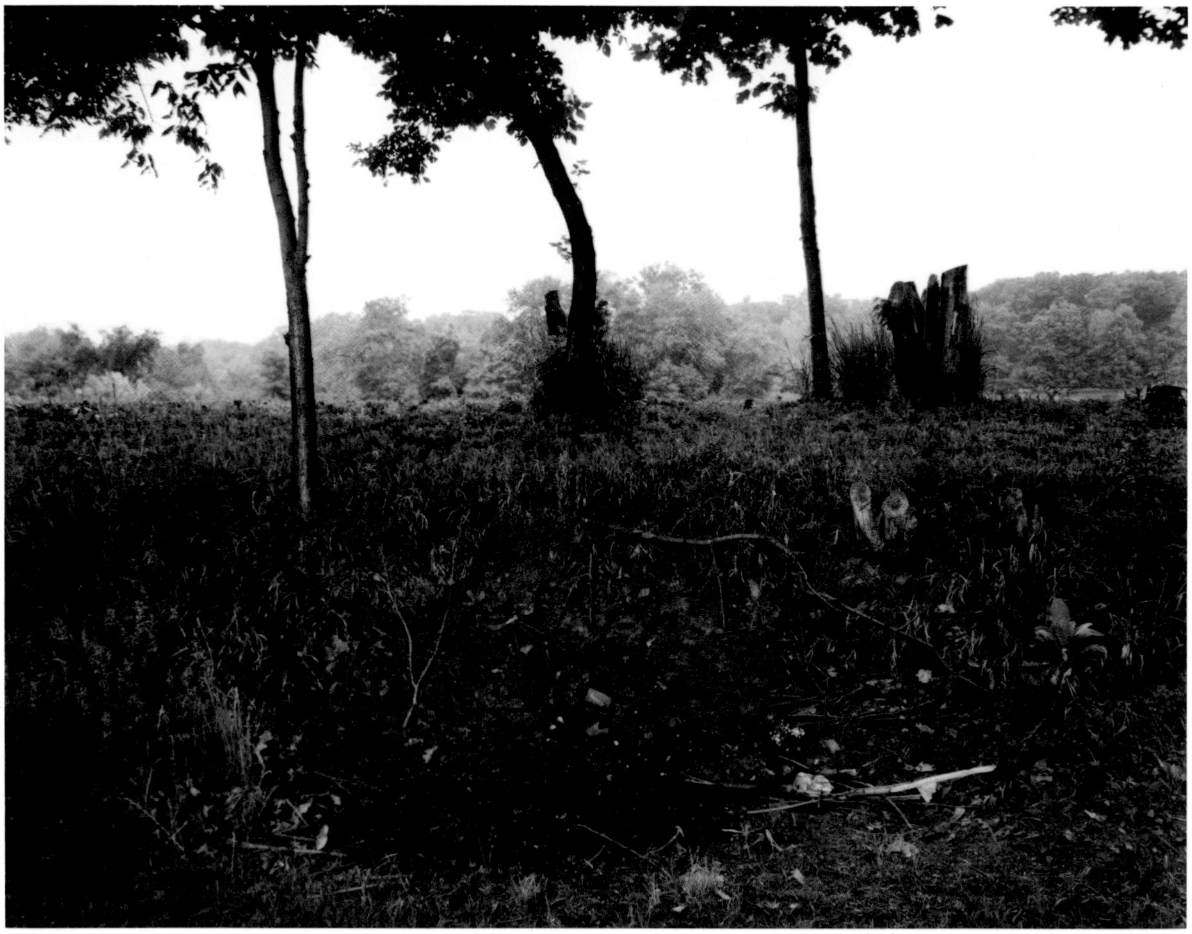

Paul, Kathryn
Richard at Lusk Creek, 1982
silver gelatin print, 233 x 326mm.
Lent by the photographer.

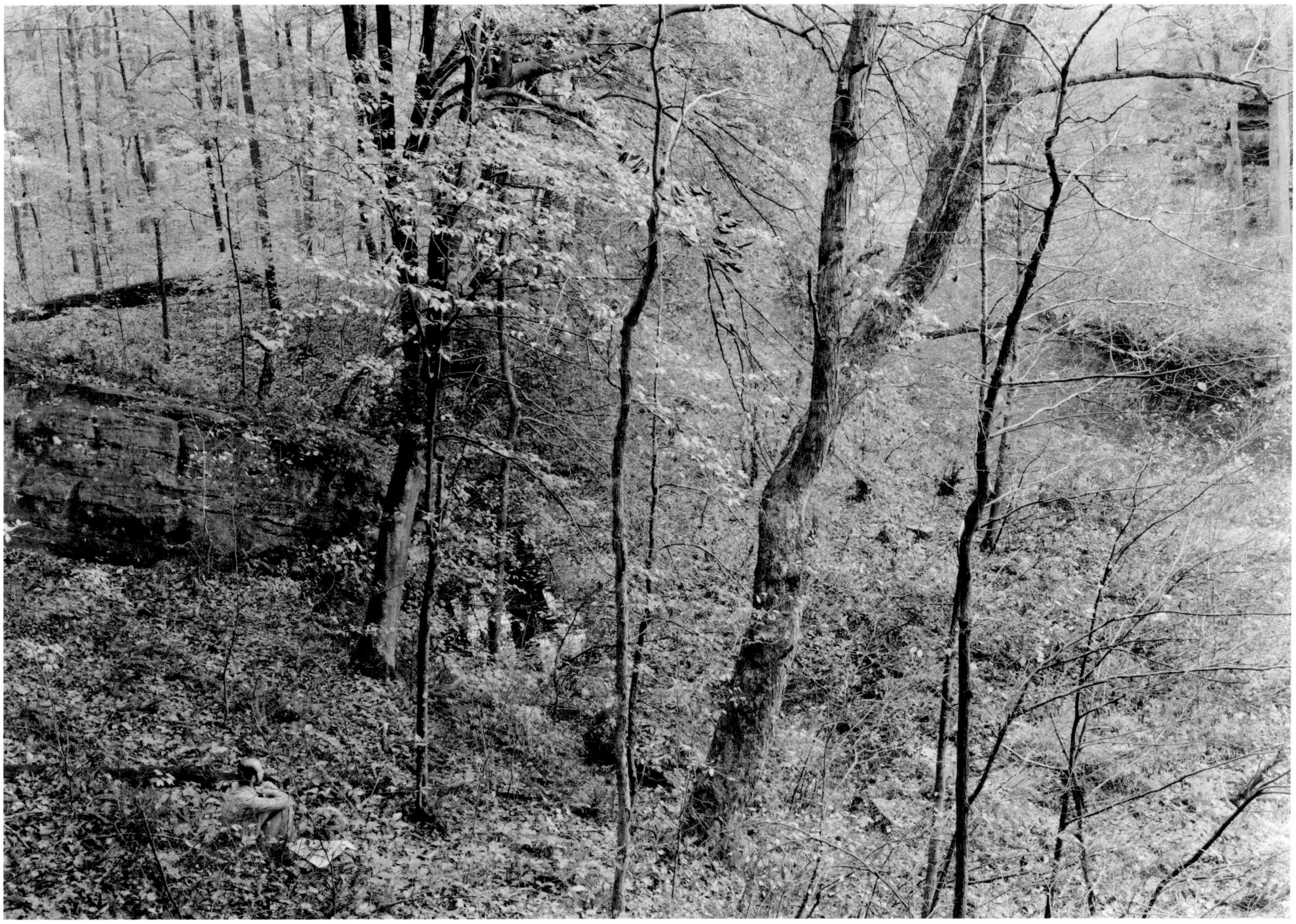

Davis, Stephen
Clay County, Minnesota, 1981
silver gelatin print, 228 x 228mm.
Lent by the photographer.

Evans, Terry
Konza Prairie Near
Manhattan, Kansas, 1982
color photograph, C-print, 229 x 229mm.
Lent by the photographer.

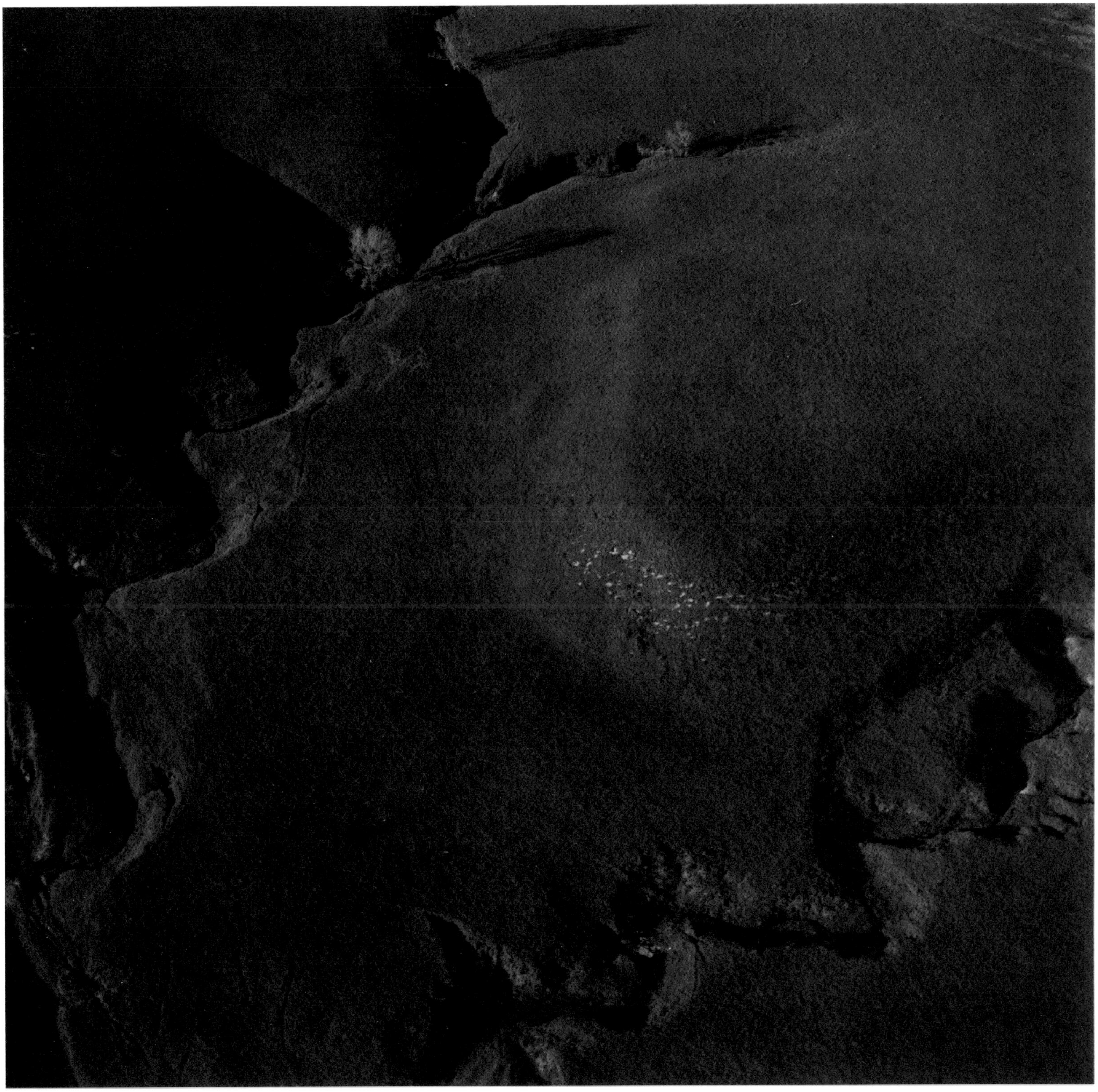

Klipper, Stuart

Farm with Elsie the Cow on the Barn, Humboldt County, Iowa, 1982
color photograph, C-print, 180 x 578mm.
Lent by the photographer.

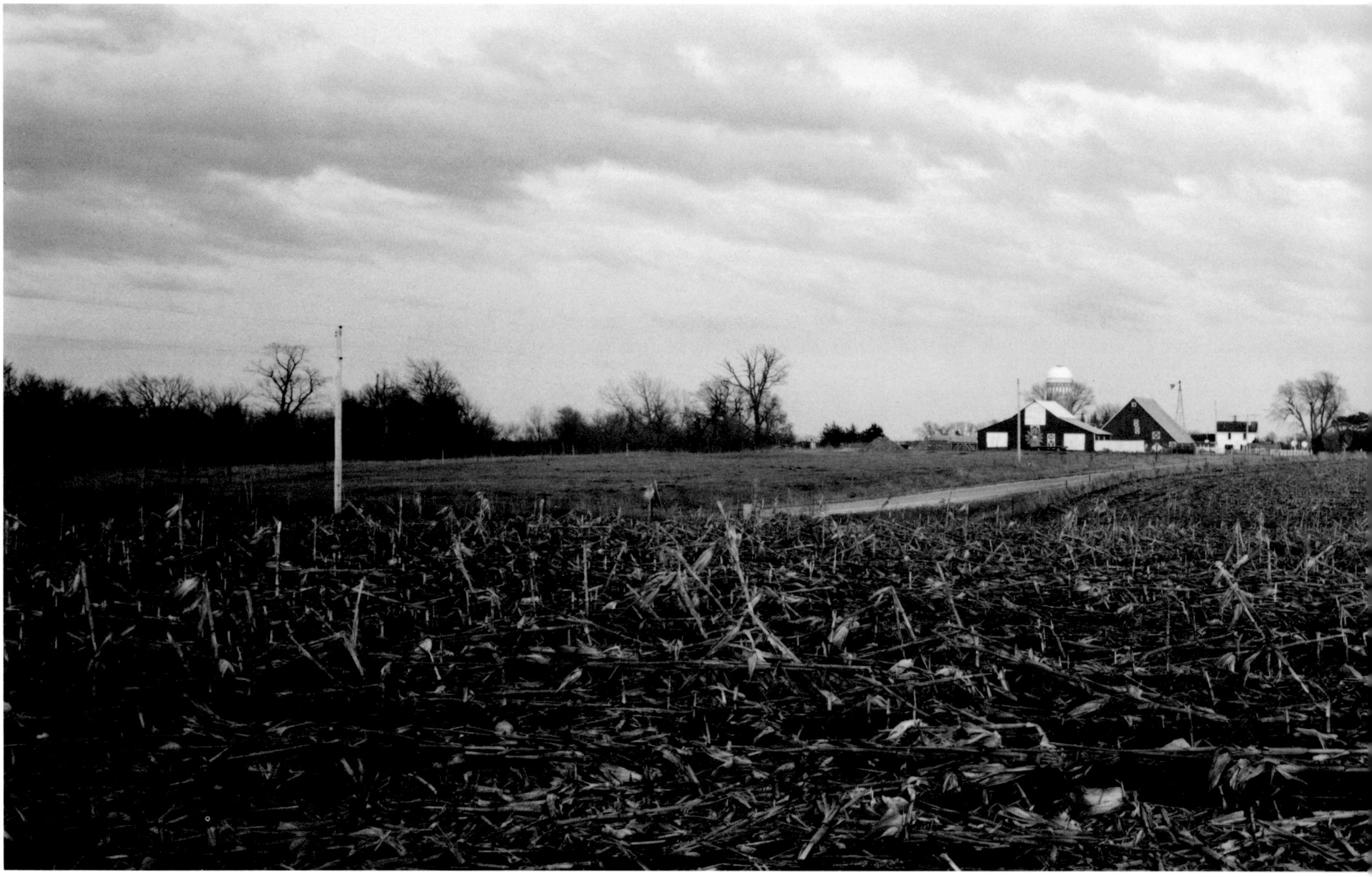

Flick, Robbert

Sequential Views, "North of Kankakee, Illinois," 1981
silver gelatin prints, 354 x 544mm.
Lent by the photographer and Tortue Gallery of Santa Monica, California.

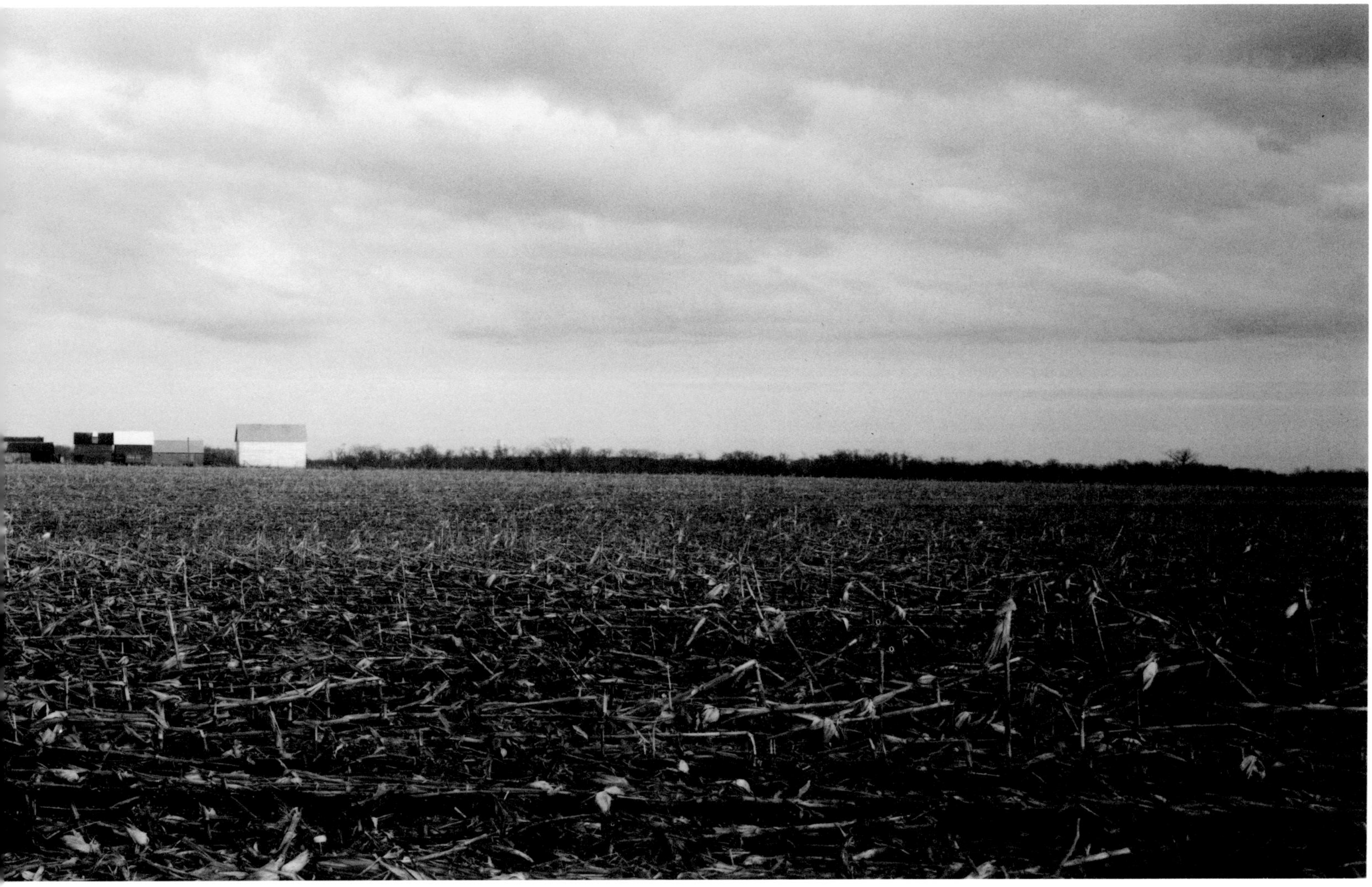

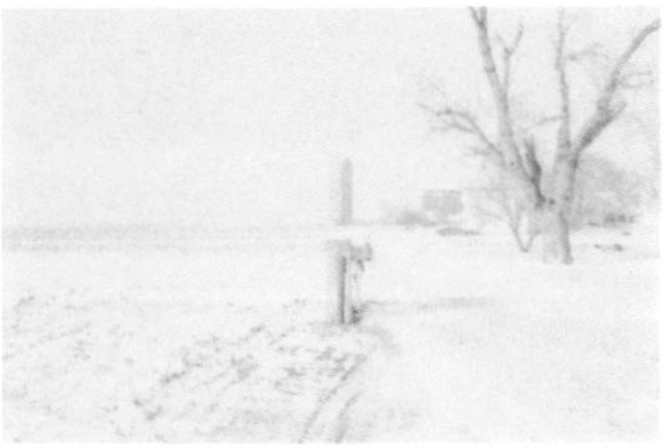
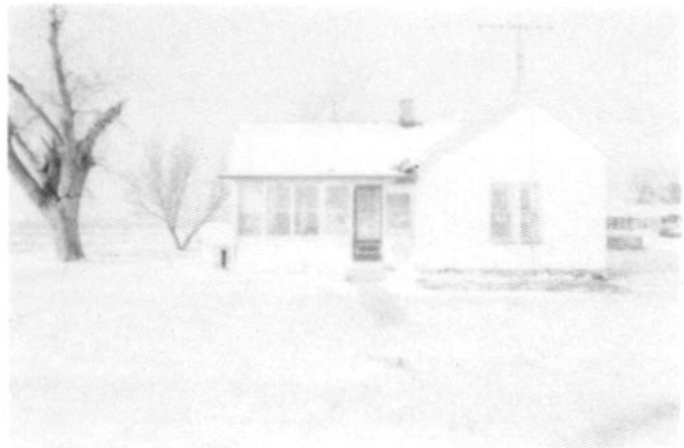
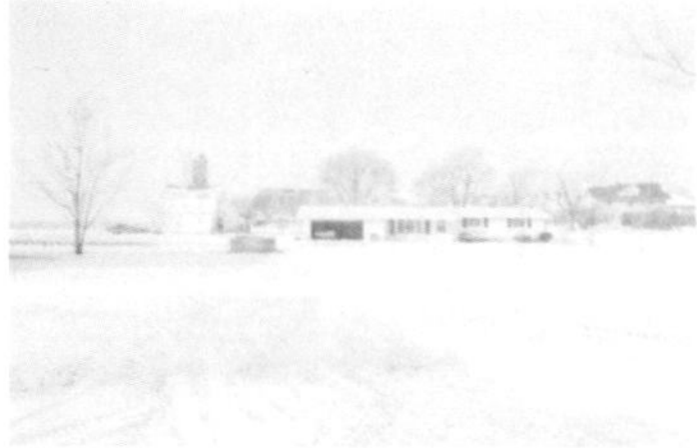
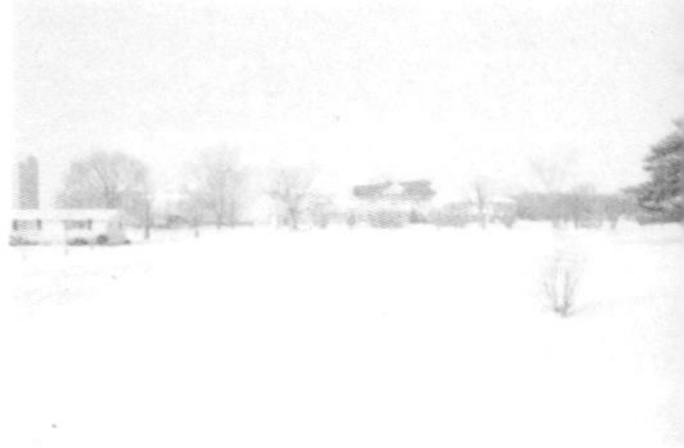

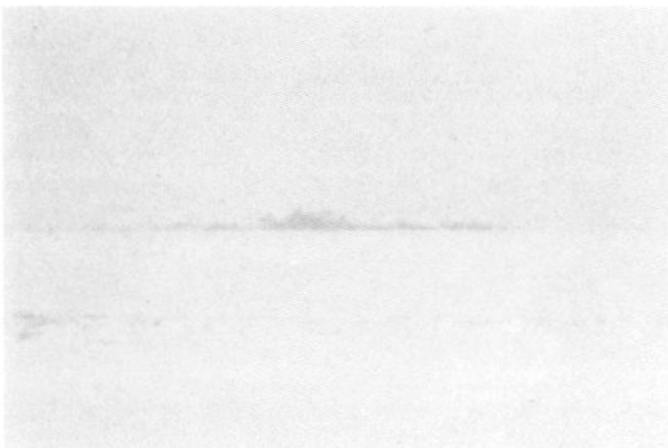

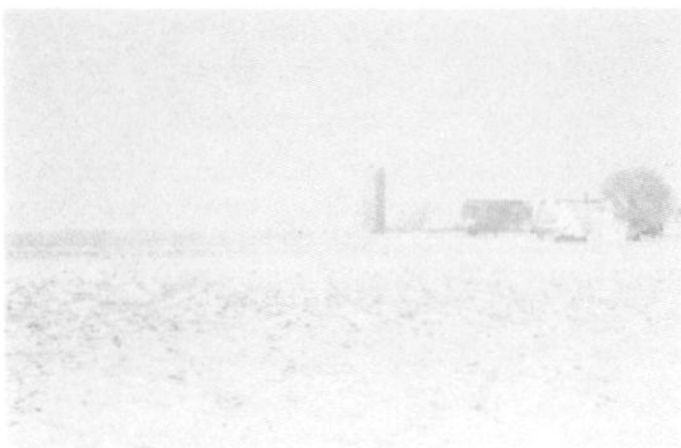
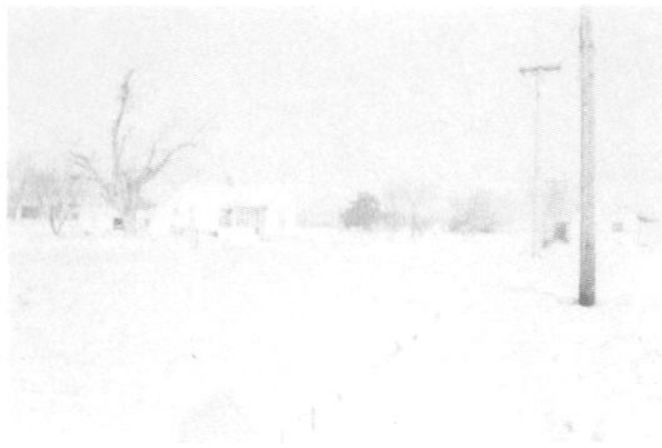

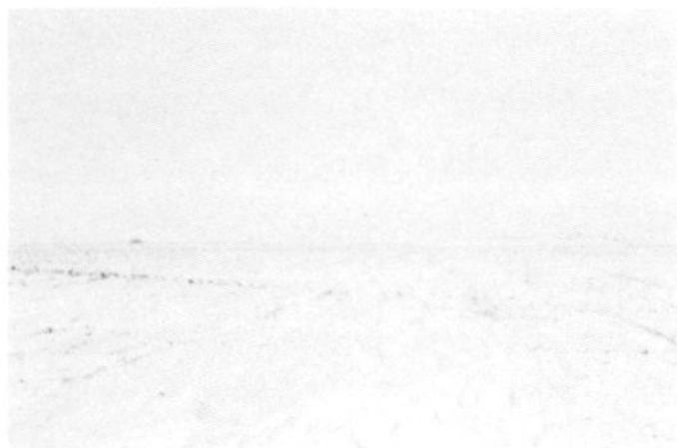

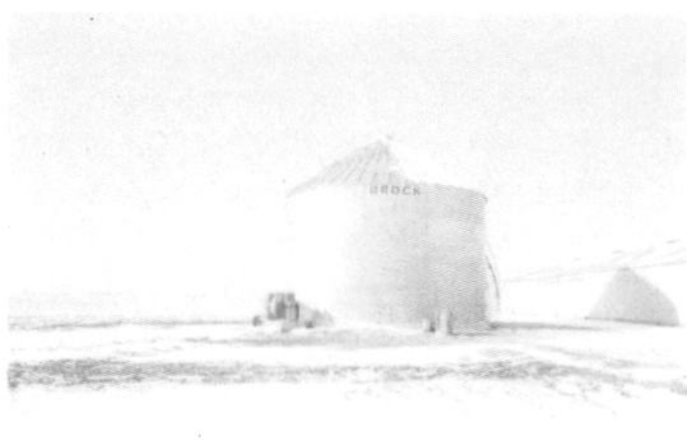
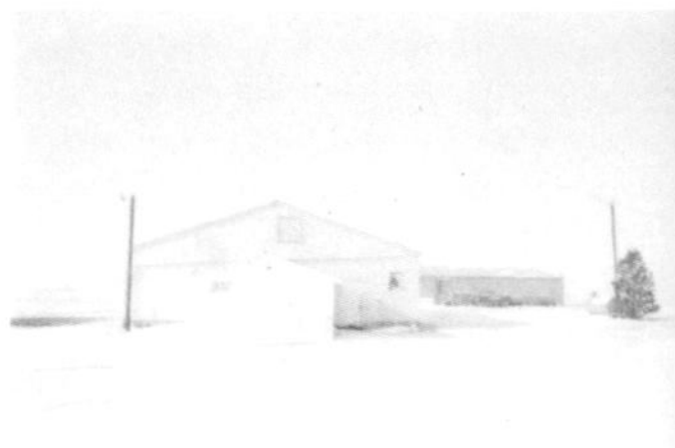

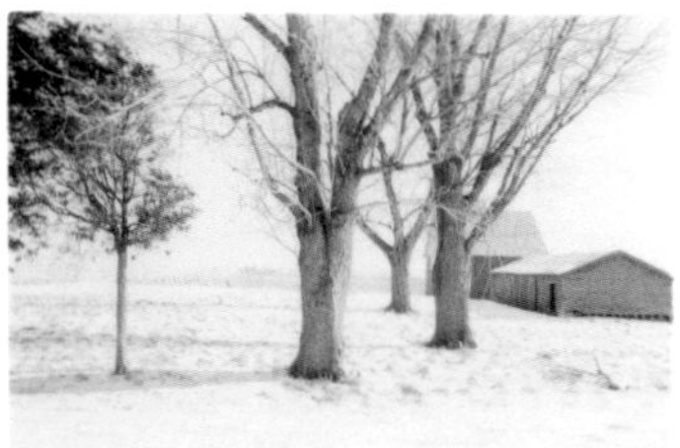
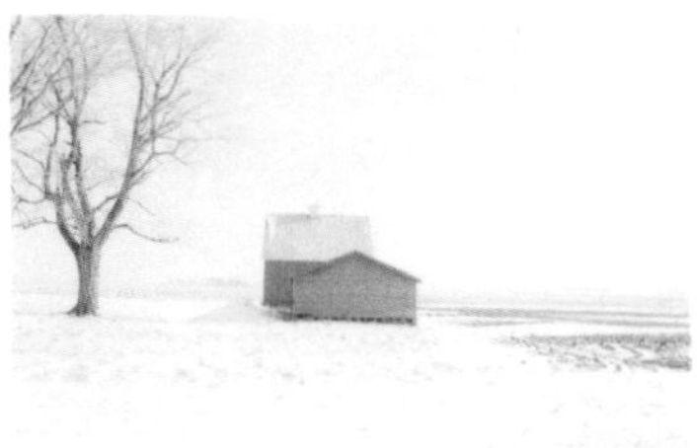

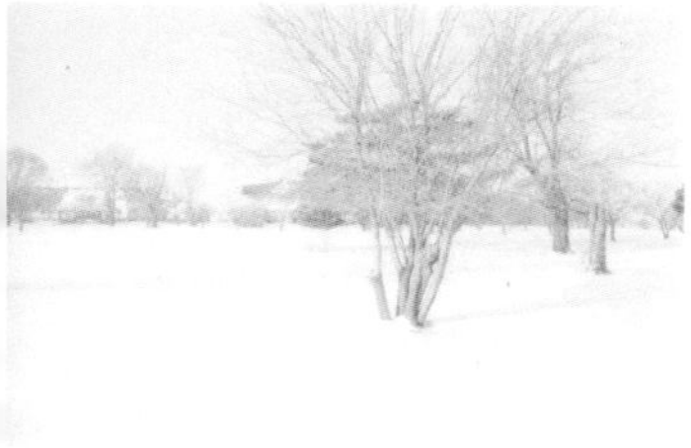
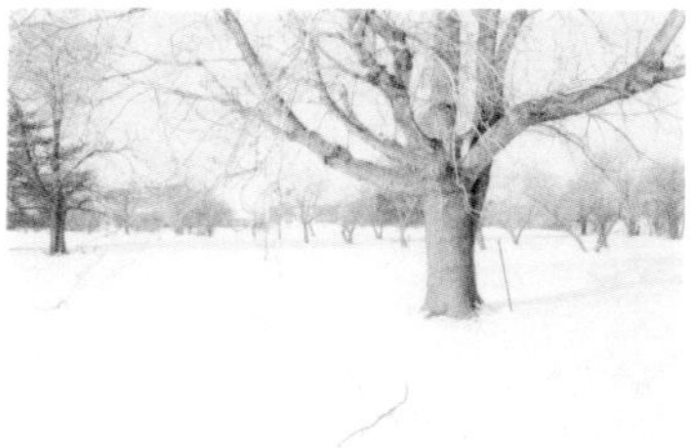
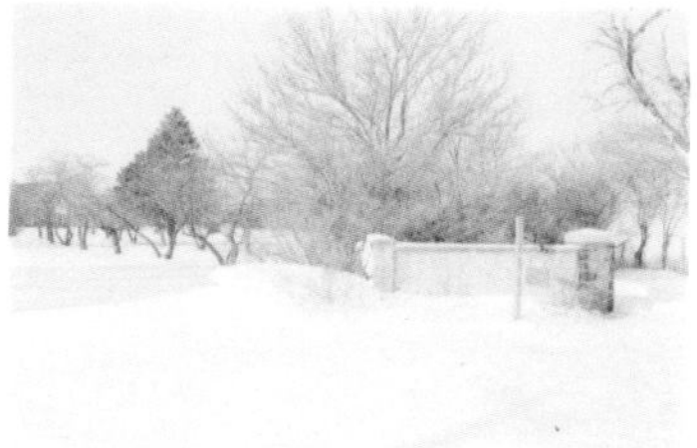
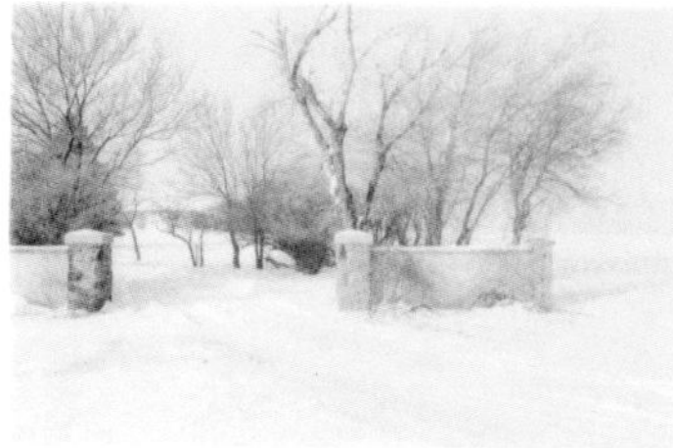
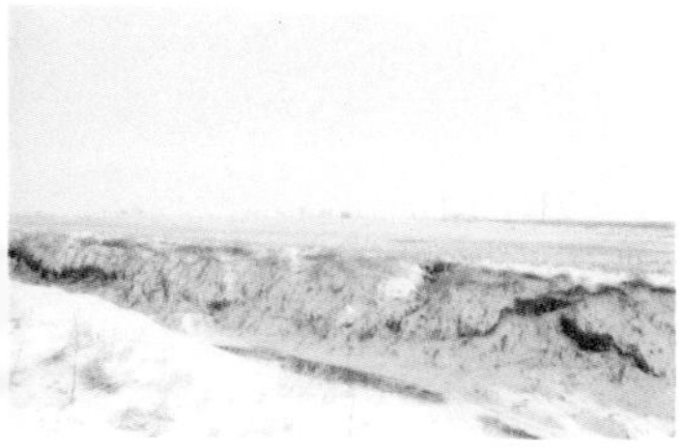
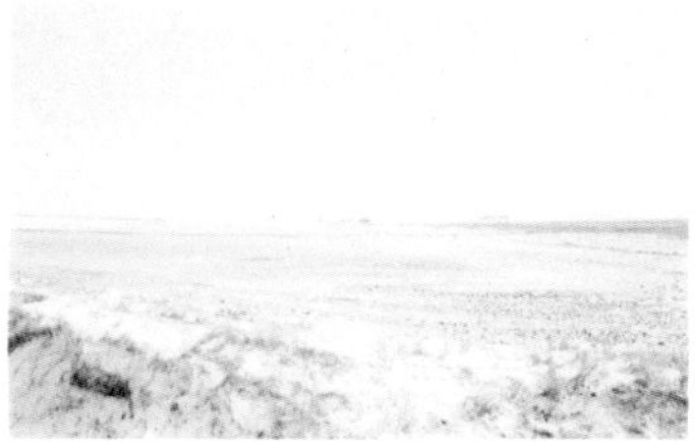
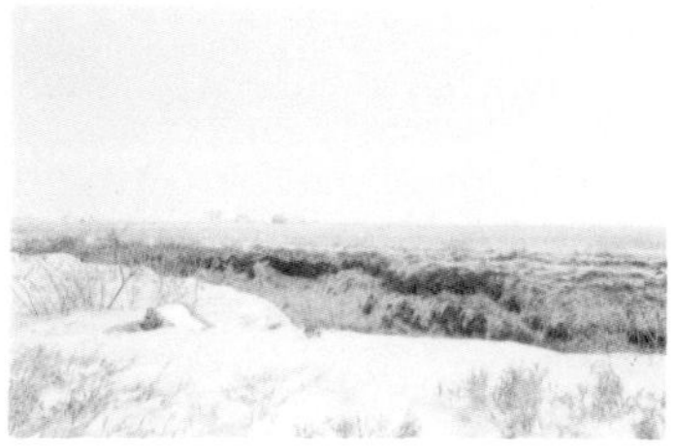
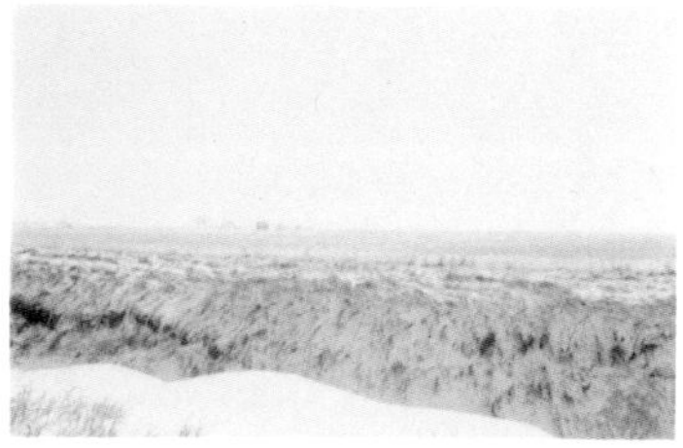

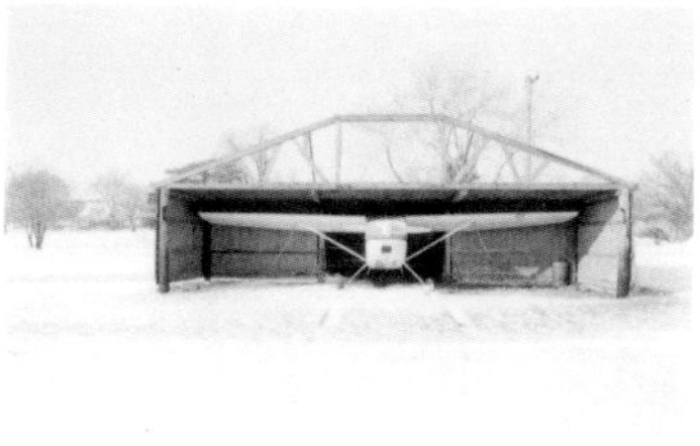

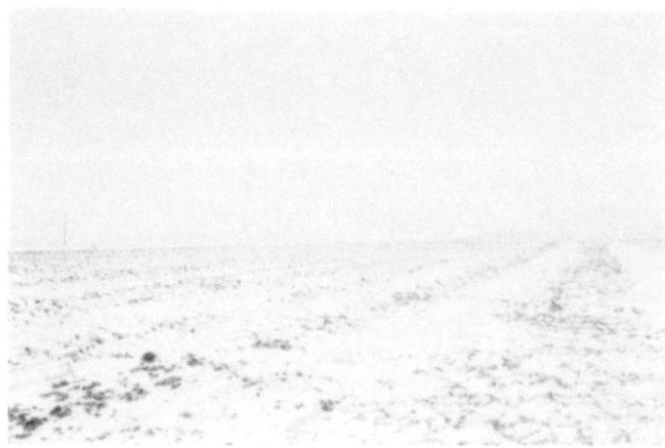

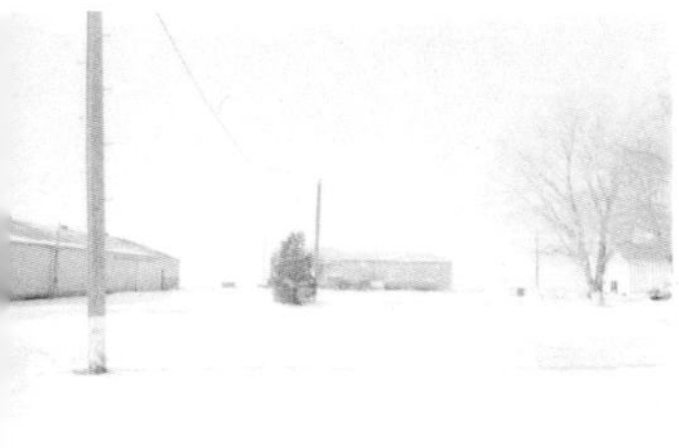
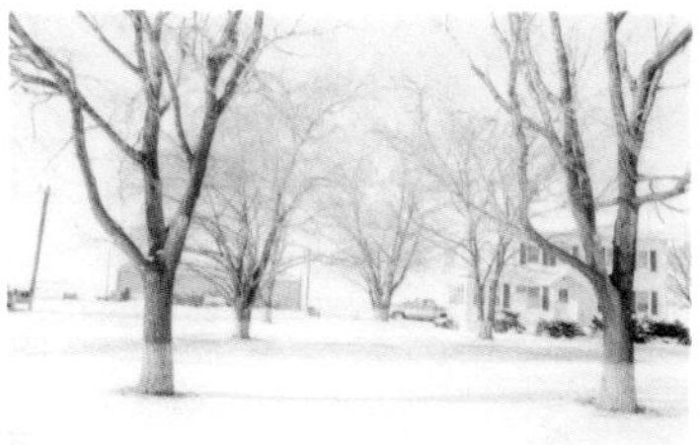
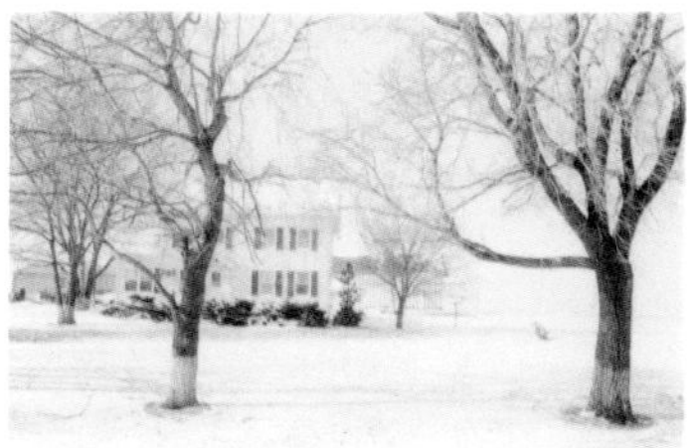
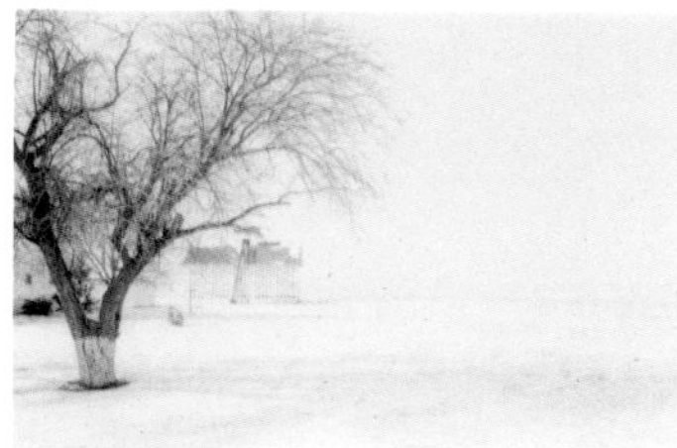
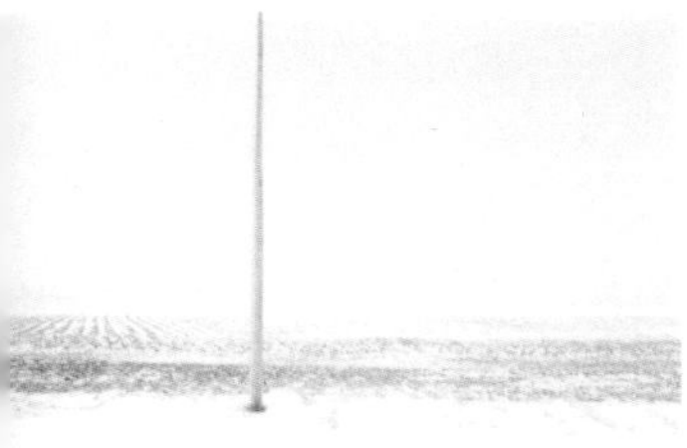
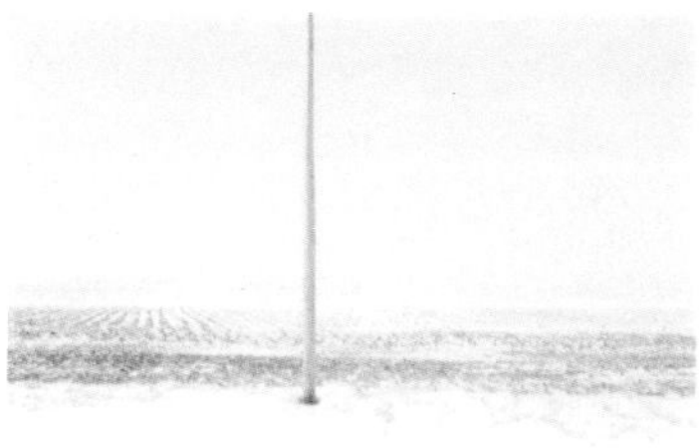

McKinney, Rhondal
Illinois Landscape, 1979
silver gelatin print, 190 x 240mm.
Lent by the photographer.

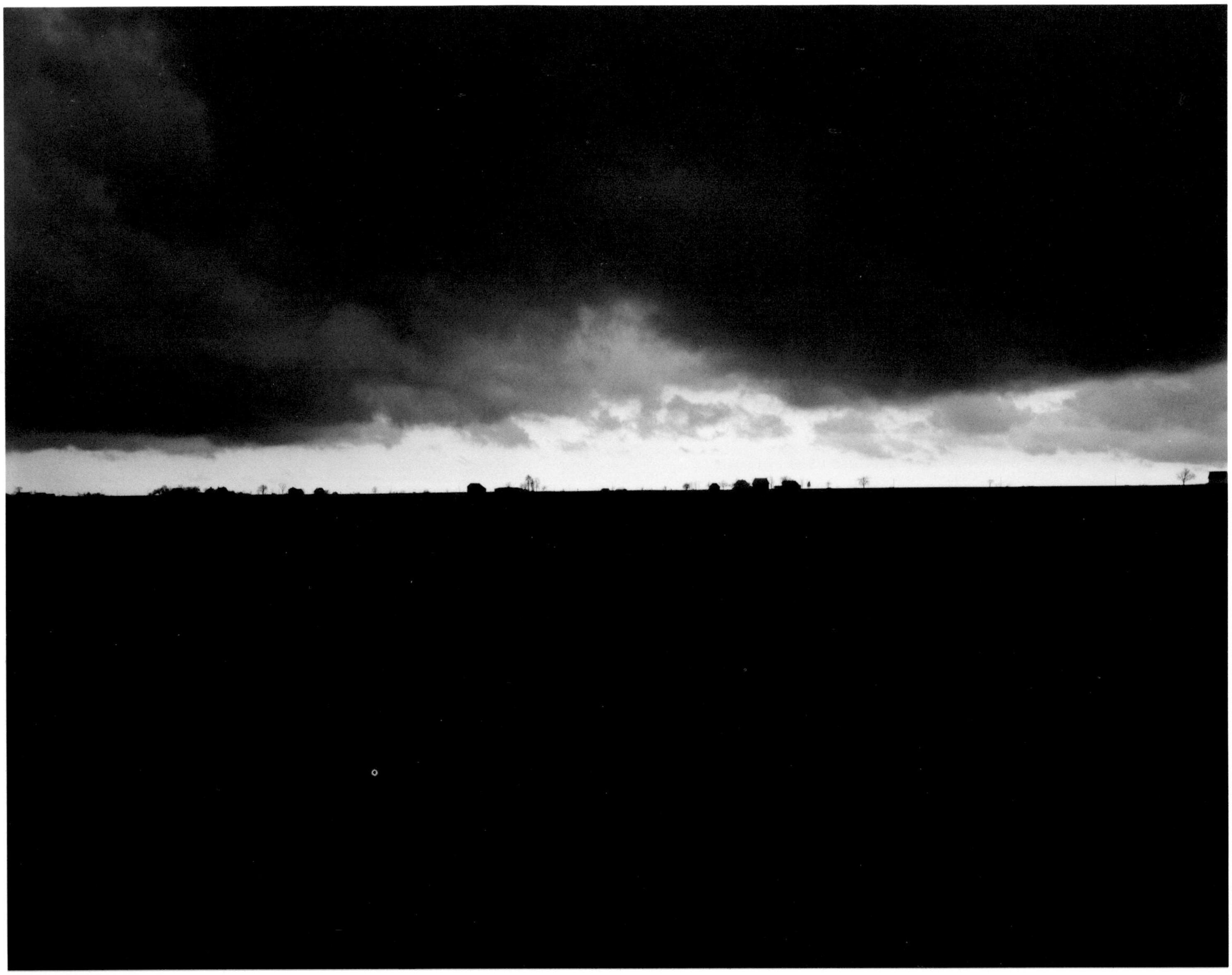

McKinney, Rhondal
Illinois Landscape, 1982
silver gelatin print, 190 x 240mm.
Lent by the photographer.

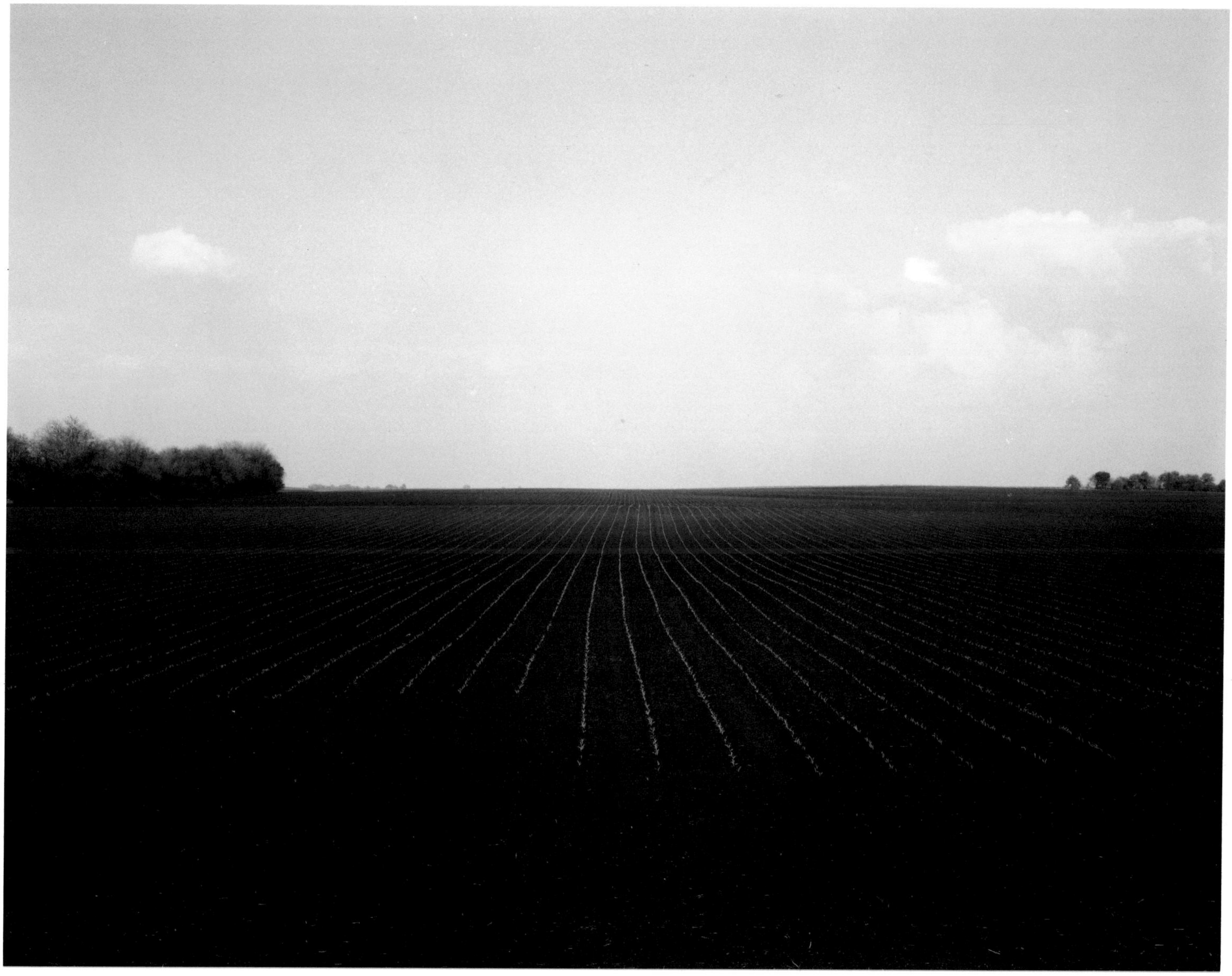

THE PRAIRIE SPIRIT

by Stephen F. Christy

I was born on the prairie and the milk of its wheat, the red of its clover, the eyes of its women, gave me a song and a slogan.

Here the water went down, the icebergs slid with gravel, the gaps and the valleys hissed, and the black loam came, and the yellow sandy loam.

Here between the sheds of the Rocky Mountains and the Appalachians, here now a morning star fixes a fire sign over the timber claims and cow pastures, the corn belt, the cotton belt, the cattle ranches.

Here the gray geese go five hundred miles and back with a wind under their wings honking the cry for a new home.

Here I know I will hanker after nothing so much as one more sunrise or a sky moon of fire doubled to a river moon of water.

The prairie sings to me in the forenoon and I know in the night I rest easy in the prairie arms, on the prairie heart.

Carl Sandburg, "Prairie"

America grew up on the prairies. When explorers and pioneers first ventured into Indiana's tallgrass meadows in the early 1800's, the United States was a sparsely settled nation with little power. By the time the last high plains were tamed in the 1890's this country was poised on a new era of global recognition. Between these times a flood of settlers poured over this vast grassland, shaping it to their ways. In doing so they very nearly destroyed its original beauty which so deeply moved early visitors. Yet the prairies, in their physical passing away, found a permanent place in the midwest soul, spawning an artistic movement which captured the creative minds of a generation. And, although obscured in recent decades, the prairie landscape and spirit is today attracting renewed interest and affection. This essay will trace the passing of the prairie landscape from a physical reality, now largely destroyed, into a spiritual expression which has flourished in the hearts and minds of midwest people and, lately, shows signs of returning in its former glory.

Despite the hardships of frontier life, early east coast settlers could count on one landscape feature familiar to their European backgrounds: trees. The vast forests of eastern America were comfortingly similar to those in Europe. Their toils and bounties were predictable: the huge trees took great efforts to remove for agriculture, but once they were down they provided raw materials for shelter, heat, and general farm use.

The settlers knew the burdens and rewards of staking out a claim in the forest. They were prepared for the challenge both physically and mentally from generations of experience in the Old World. The forest itself provided shelter and protection, particularly after the Indians had left, and a homestead or community became a civilized island nestled in a sea of trees. And, most importantly, the settlers could control the scale of their landscape by removing trees to provide openness and closure, sun and shade, as they might wish. They were in control of their surroundings.

All this changed abruptly in the last century. Word began to circulate back East of a vast treeless landscape in America's center. Westward pressing settlers, accustomed to generations of forest life, stumbled blinking into this sunlit land. It was unlike anything they had ever seen. Momentarily confused, they clung to its forested edges. Yet within 100 years they had conquered it, forever altering its original scope and brilliance.

What was this prairie landscape? Passing in a huge arc from the eastern Rockies through Oklahoma to western Ohio, it was a strange, largely treeless landscape dominated by grasses and flowers unknown in the colonial United States. In its rich eastern section, extending roughly from Iowa, Missouri, and Minnesota to Indiana, it contained grasses whose height often exceeded that of a person on horseback. Below this area lay some of the richest soils in the world, the result of earlier glacial action and centuries of rampant prairie growth and decay. Farther west the grasses became shorter and the soils thinner as the land's elevation rose to meet the Rockies. These areas were known as middlegrass and shortgrass prairies. They differed markedly from their richer eastern counterparts, which enjoyed a more moist and temperate climate from the Gulf of Mexico. The combination of abundant rainfall, moderate temperatures, and rich soils destined the tallgrass prairie to become America's bread basket.

Fire maintained the prairie and was the grassland's single greatest ally in holding its own against the forests, which constantly struggled to invade the prairies from the relative safety of most river bottoms and valleys. Whether started by natural causes such as lightning, or by human interference such as blazes set by Indians to drive game, these fires were the life blood of the prairie. Unlike trees or shrubs, which though dormant in the winter are still alive both above and below ground, prairie grasses and flowers die back completely above ground after each growing season. In the fall their life force retreats into their roots, which often extend fifteen feet down into the ground.

In late fall and early spring their dead dry foliage above ground thus became perfect tinder for fires. Once started these fires would travel for miles, often driven by strong winds at a pace faster than a person could run. The fires did no harm to the prairie, which lay dormant in the cool earth below, or to its animals, which could outrun the flames or scamper to safety in their burrows and dens. Indeed the prairies' nutrients were recycled in the ashes, whose black color helped capture the warmth of the spring sun and hasten new growth. There were and are few sights as beautiful as the fresh spring growth on a just-burned prairie. Every flower and blade of grass is completely new, its colors undiluted by the dull browns of last year's leaves and chaff.

But for the forestland trees and shrubs, eager to invade these open areas, the results were disastrous. Early settlers often reported passing through hundreds of yards of charred and dead woodlands on the ever-changing edge where prairie and forest met. Back and forth this ecological battle waged, with both prairie and forest taking and losing ground over the centuries.

The astonishment our forest-bred forebears felt when first meeting the prairie rings loudly in their early journals. It is our loss that these early impressions, formed in the 1820's to the 1840's, predate the general use of the camera by so agonizingly short a time. Thus words alone must capture the marvel of this untouched land; but the verbal descriptions foreshadow how perfectly the prairies were suited to the photographer's art.

Traveling through the woodlands of eastern Indiana, one settler recorded his first entry onto a prairie. His remarks are worth noting in full because they span the wide range of feelings commonly experienced by people unprepared for what they saw.

> Bruised by the brushwood and exhausted by the extreme heat we almost despaired, when a small cabin and a low fence greeted our eyes. A few steps more, and a beautiful prairie suddenly opened to view.
>
> At first, we only received the impression of its general beauty. With longer gaze, all its distinctive features were revealed, lying in profound repose under the warm light of an afternoon's summer sun. Its indented and irregular outline of wood, its varied surface interspersed with clumps of oaks of centuries' growth, its tall grass, with seed stalks from six to ten feet high, like tall and slender reeds waving in a gentle breeze, the whole presenting a magnificence of park scenery, complete from the hand of Nature, and unrivalled by the same sort of scenery by European art.
>
> For once, the reality came up to the picture of imagination. Our station was in the wood, on rising ground; from it, a descent of about a hundred yards to the valley of the prairie, about a quarter of a mile wide, extending to the base of a majestic slope, rising upward for a full half-mile, crowned by groves of noble oaks. A little to the left the eye wandered up a long stretch of prairie for three miles, into which projected hills and slopes, covered with rich grass and half-grown trees, from four to eight in a clump.
>
> After traveling from the Atlantic shore to the Wabash River, a thousand miles of gloomy forest, or running the length of the Ohio and Mississippi rivers, with a prospect ever bounded by impenetrable foliage, the entrance into one of these beautiful and light expanses of verdure is most enchanting, the beautifully indented outlines of woods and the undulating surface of the prairie affording innumerable sites for tasteful dwellings, the ornamental clumps of full-grown oaks scattered by the hand of nature so that they defy imitation by art, the bright verdure, rich herbage, affording food for innumerable flocks and herds, the beautiful flowers, the transparent atmosphere, the soft zephyrs wafted from the South in bland and rich volume, all combine to impress the enchanted beholder with pleased feelings, even to delusion.[1]

Another early visitor described how deeply moving the newness of these prairies was:

> In their irregular outline of woodland and their undulating surfaces, these tracts of natural meadow exhibit every beauty, fresh from the hand of nature, which art often labors in vain to produce; but there are no organs of perception, no faculties as yet prepared in this country, for the enjoyment of these exquisite combinations.[2]

Indeed, the first observers had no "faculties" with which to describe these prairies in familiar terms. The closest writers could come was to liken the prairies to English landscape parks, a familiar metaphor to their eastern audiences.

---

1. George Flower, History of the English Settlement, (1817), as quoted in John Madson, Where the Sky Began, p. 12.
2. Morris Birkbeck, "Notes from Shawneetown," (1817), as quoted in Walter Havighurst, Land of the Long Horizons, p. 151.

The bounding forest projected and receded in pleasing forms, and the distant outlines appeared graceful...perhaps conceptions of beauty and grouping trees, formed in the artificial school of Britain, are inapplicable to the magnificent scale on which nature hath adorned the country between Springfield and Chicago. The works of man are mere distortions compared with those of nature, and I have no doubt many prairies, containing hundreds of square miles, exceed the finest English parks in beauty....[3]

More telling, however, were the metaphors that spoke directly to the emotions without the aid of artistic or intellectual descriptions, and here we find the early writers closely approaching the photographer's art. Time and again the descriptions liken the prairies to a sea. One writer noticed how clumps of trees stood out in the prairie "like islands in the ocean."[4] Another described Iowa in 1839:

These plains, although preserving a general level in respect to the whole country, are yet in themselves not flat, but exhibit a graceful waving surface, swelling and sinking with an easy slope and full rounded outline...It is that surface, which, in the expressive language of the country, is called rolling, and which has been said to resemble the long, heavy swell of the ocean when its waves are subsiding to rest after the agitation of a storm.[5]

The oceanic feeling people often felt in these prairies created irrational experiences. Just as at sea, perceptions became distorted and logic thwarted:

I now found the truth of what I had read about the difficulty of distinguishing distances on a prairie. The feeling is quite bewildering. A man walking near looks like a Goliath a mile off. I mistook a covered wagon without horses, at a distance of fifty yards, for a white house near the horizon...[6]

Descriptions like these abound, all revealing that the newly-discovered prairies were extraordinary, deeply moving experiences. Life on them was difficult, to be sure, and many early writers chronicle the grim side of Midwest settlement. What concerns us here, though, is the presence of a spirit of a new landscape and the deep impression it made on its settlers. Those who stayed grew to love it and prospered from its richness. Yet in doing so they destroyed it.

A thousand red men cried and went away to new places for corn and women: a million white men came and put up skyscrapers, threw out rails and wires, feelers to the salt sea: now the smokestacks bite the skyline with stub teeth.
—Carl Sandburg, "Prairie."

No landscape was more susceptible to alteration than the prairies. For a while these lands remained untouched due to the popular belief that the absence of trees indicated soils too poor to farm—a reasonable assumption based on previous experiences with isolated "barrens" in Kentucky, Ohio, and elsewhere, whose dry sandy soil supported only grasses.

Gradually word got around that the prairies embraced the best soils, and from that moment on their destruction was assured. The land was literally ready for the taking, having already been cleared of trees and stones by nature's glaciers and fires:

Let the New England farmer who has spent half of his life in gathering the stones and grubbing the stumps out of a five-acre lot, and the other half trying to make lean, jaundiced corn grow in the two inches of soil, come out and look upon these cornfields of hundreds of acres, where the rich black loam is turned up by the plow to a depth of two feet, where is never seen a stick or a stone...[7]

Breaking the thick prairie sod was a difficult and expensive task, but John Deere's mass introduction of the steel plow in the 1840's overcame that problem. The end of the prairie was in sight as settlers streamed across it and took their claims.

Between the Civil War and the turn of the century nearly all tallgrass prairie vanished. The lush grasses were plowed under and the magnificent fires which sustained the prairies could no longer migrate at will. These awesome and frightening sights fast became a memory; soon few could recall, as one early traveller had, a prairie fire by the light of which

...we could read fine print for ½ a mile or more. And the light reflected from the cloud of smoke enlightened our road for miles after the blaze of the fire was out of sight.[8]

---

3. Patrick Shirreff, "Peoria, Pekin, Springfield, and the Prairies," (1833), as quoted in Paul Angle, Prairie State, p. 132.

4. Shirreff, ibid., p. 133.

5. James Hall, "Plumbe's Sketches," (1839), in Madson, op. cit., p. 14.

6. Harriet Martineau, "The Prairies and Joliet," (1836), in Angle, op. cit., p. 174.

7. J. P. Thompson, "River Travel, Peoria, Jacksonville, and Prairie Farming," (1851), in Angle, ibid., p. 265.

With the passing of fire the ecological balance tipped in favor of trees and brush, and within a generation many former prairies had become small forests. In addition the native grasses could not compete with the aggressive farmstead plants brought by the settlers. One writer noted this change succinctly:

Indigenous plants and grasses retire before those introduced by man; just as the Indians retire before the white man.[9]

Thus within several generations the original tallgrass prairie vanished. What seems strange in retrospect is how complete the destruction was and little-mourned was this passing. Only a few people lamented the change from grassland to cropland:

Cultivation, too, has sadly marred the effect of these [prairies]; one can scarcely conceive how much the sight of a distant corn patch, or field of wheat, or even a fence, or inclosure round a dwelling, takes away from the aspect of romantic wildness usually associated with the idea of a prairie of the West.[10]

What a grandparent remembered as reality became to the grandchild only fantasy. The prairie, with its "romantic wilderness," was gone.

Yet in this great transformation the prairie took root in the midwestern soul. While giving up physical ground it gained great spiritual ground. Even in its passing it took on new life in the imagination and dreams, forming and shaping a midwest consciousness. This consciousness finally flowered into art with the birth of the Prairie School.

The rise of this school and its creations, particularly by architects, corresponded with the vanishing of the original prairies around 1900. It held sway in Illinois, Minnesota, Iowa and Wisconsin for the next twenty years. The Prairie School was, and remains, the greatest tribute to the beauty of middle America. A critic described its elements thus in 1918:

In imitation of a certain broad and horizontal disposition of lines individually employed, a school of design has sprung up for which its authors claim the title "American." The horizontal lines of the new expression appeal to the disciples of this school as echoing the spirit of the prairies of the great Middle West, which to them embodies the essence of democracy.[11]

The works of Louis Sullivan and Frank Lloyd Wright best epitomize the efforts of this great school. Wright first crystallized the movement in his 1901 article in Ladies' Home Journal describing and illustrating "A Home in a Prairie Town":

...the exterior recognizes the influence of the prairie, is firmly and broadly associated with the site, and makes a feature of its quiet level. The low terraces and broad eaves are designed to accentuate the quiet level and complete the harmonious relationship.[12]

Thus had the idea and spirit of the prairie entered midwest civilization and borne artistic fruit. Yet this fruit needed appreciation and acceptance in order to become widespread. Here again the power of the midwest landscape had worked itself on the minds of men and women. Prairie School clients were the first generation of people who had grown up in the Midwest. They did not languish for the tastes and conventions of the East as had earlier generations. America was young and still regionally oriented, and east coast esthetics seemed far away. Wright drew his early clients chiefly from

...American men of business with unspoiled instincts and ideas. A man of this type usually has the faculty of judging for himself...[M]uch of the encouragement this work receives comes straight from him because the "common sense" of the thing appeals to him.[13]

Artist and client thus collaborated to bring into society the beauty of the recently-vanished prairie. The key element was the capturing not of the original prairie landscape, since this was fast disappearing, but rather what came to be known as the "prairie spirit." These artists—not just architects, but writers, sculptors, poets, and landscape architects as well—sought to capture and express the beauty of the midwest landscape that had flowered in their souls.

8. Alfred Brunson, "A Prairie Fire and a Claim Association," (1835), in Angle, ibid., p. 162.

9. William Ferguson, "Through Illinois on the Illinois Central," (1855), in Angle, ibid., p. 300.

10. Elizabeth Ellet, "By Rail and Stage To Galena," (1852), in Angle, ibid., pp. 272-273.

11. Irving Pond, "The Meaning of Architecture," (1918), as quoted from Allen Brooks, The Prairie School, p. 5.

12. F. L. Wright, "A Home in a Prairie Town," (1901), as quoted in Elizabeth Howett, "Frank Lloyd Wright and American Residential Landscaping," Landscape, Vol. 26, #1, p. 34.

13. F. L. Wright, as quoted in Brooks, op. cit., p. 16.

Landscape architects in particular went a long way toward creating this vision, often collaborating with Prairie School architects to tie together buildings and grounds. In the 1870's Ossian Simonds first noticed the beauty of the vanishing prairie in the hawthorns, wild plums, and other native trees and shrubs which for centuries had grown along the rich edges where prairie and forest met. He took these materials and made Chicago's Graceland Cemetery, for which he was the landscape gardener, into a beauty spot renowned throughout the Midwest. He later transformed the parks of Quincy, Illinois, in similar manner.

Yet it remained for Danish-born landscape architect Jens Jensen to draw the clearest picture of the prairie spirit on public and private grounds. His work was the main inspiration behind a University of Illinois publication entitled The Prairie Spirit in Landscape Gardening. Issued in 1915, this manifesto pointed out that landscape architecture must not only provide people with recreation and pleasure but also "inspire them with the vanished beauty of the prairie."[14] It allied itself closely with the Prairie School:

> The prairie style of landscape gardening is an American mode of design based upon the practical needs of the middle-western people and characterized by the preservation of typical western scenery, by restoration of local color, and by repetition of the horizontal line of land or sky which is the strongest feature of prairie scenery.[15]

The publication also advocated the establishment of what it called "prairie parks":

> ...every middle western state will make one prairie reservation before it is too late or recreate one wild prairie for the people to enjoy forever...a prairie park might touch a very responsive chord in the popular heart and sight to win the everlasting gratitude of mankind.[16]

Jens Jensen epitomized all these ideals. He had an extensive practice that embraced numerous clients who were often sympathetic to the Prairie School. As landscape architect for Chicago's West Parks, he rebuilt them into visions capturing the essence of the midwest landscape. His simple and clean design for the enormous conservatory in Garfield Park, for instance, sprang directly from his appreciation of dome-shaped haystacks once seen on a flat Nebraska field. Columbus Park, his greatest public work, was recognized nationwide as an outstanding artistic effort. Furthermore, Jensen's dynamic presence and stature played a great part in the establishment of larger public landscapes such as the forest preserves around Chicago and the state park systems of Illinois, Indiana, and Wisconsin. Everywhere he applied his maxim for design and art:

> There is beauty everywhere in America, but we look across the seas for something we will never get. Whatever will fit the America of tomorrow must be an outgrowth of the American soil.[17]

Jensen, Wright, Sullivan, Simonds and many others all sensed the power and mystery of the middle American landscape and interpreted it through their works. They gave expression and character to midwest civilization by revealing through art the potent force of the prairies which had shaped America's heartland. Their art expressed an ideal, for the true prairie landscape continued to vanish as the twentieth century grew older.

Worse still, after the First World War the Prairie School itself faltered and vanished. Many reasons have been cited for this, but the chief one seems to have been a loss of the regionalism which had made America so diverse and special. The war had united the country and firmly centered the nation's power in the East. People began to look again to the East for style and taste. The lavish spending of the 1920's, coupled with a war-time sympathy for Britain and France, revived interest in Colonial and period architecture. Conformity became the rule, and regionalism was dead.

> I speak of new cities and new people.
> I tell you the past is a bucket of ashes.
> I tell you yesterday is a wind gone down, a sun dropped in the west.
> I tell you there is nothing in the world only an ocean of tomorrows, a sky of tomorrows.
> I am a brother of the cornhuskers who say at sundown:
> Tomorrow is a day.
> —Carl Sandburg, "Prairie"

---

14. Wilhelm Miller, "The Prairie Spirit in Landscape Gardening," (1915), p. 1.

15. Ibid., p. 5

16. Ibid., p. 7

17. "Finds Art in Clean Yards," Chicago Daily News, May 9, 1943.

The next three decades witnessed a gradual loss of the midwest landscape from public consciousness. Certainly the great stands of middlegrass and tallgrass prairie had long since vanished, and during the boom years of the 1920's much shortgrass prairie fell before the plow as well. Nature retaliated with a vengeance, however, and the Dust Bowl of the Great Depression was the shortgrass prairie soils taken flight. World War II and prosperity followed, and the rich tallgrass prairie soils produced their bounty year after year. Little thought was given to their origins.

Here and there, however, interest in this landscape stayed alive. In the depths of the Depression John Curtis and Henry Greene at the University of Wisconsin began experiments to restore an original prairie. With Civilian Conservation Corps labor, Curtis combed the countryside for small untouched patches of prairie that might still exist in overlooked corners or along old roadways and railroads. Using seed and transplants, he set about recreating a piece of tallgrass prairie in an abandoned cornfield at the University's arboretum. His co-worker Greene began similar efforts on a dry pasture to the west. Neither knew much about prairie ecology. A lot of what the early settlers had seen and recorded was forgotten; Curtis and Greene were cautious at first about using fire to help their work since the idea was novel and untried. From these efforts of a half-century ago, however, sprang the beginnings of a movement which today has brought the prairie back to life for many midwesterners.

Curtis, Greene and others puttered along until the mid-1960's, when the environmental movement suddenly brought natural landscapes into the public eye. Almost overnight national organizations such as The Nature Conservancy and local efforts such as Chicago's Open Lands Project greatly expanded their search for protection of virgin land. The prairies attracted particular attention. In the middle and high plains, where the ravages of cow and plow had not been so thorough, enormous tracts such as the 7500-acre Samuel Ordway Memorial Prairie in South Dakota were created. There it is possible today to sense the quiet lonely beauty of the dry and hardy shortgrass prairie.

But in the tallgrass regions a different story unfolded. The destruction of these landscapes has been so complete that an inventory of Illinois turned up only six acres of virgin tallgrass prairie for every one million that had once existed. The great "prairie parks" that the Prairie School followers sought had never been secured, and the loss was final. Belatedly, private and public monies set aside these last few parcels. So rare are they that the public is generally restricted access; most of them are held in specially-protected nature preserves and scientific areas.

With permission a person might go and look at these jewels and, with a little imagination, see such a landscape magnified a thousand-fold. Never again, though, will any of us know the profusion of grasses and flowers that greeted the first settlers. Never will we see sunlit fogs reflecting the colors of different flower colonies as they rolled across the prairies. Never will we be able to stand, as an early traveller did, overlooking "nine miles of prairie, which we had traversed in dim moonlight last night, now exquisitely beautiful as the sun shown on them."[18]

There is hope for the future. Prairie restorations, formerly the domain of backyard landscapers or minor arboretum projects, are growing in size. At the Fermi National Accelerator Laboratory outside of Chicago an enterprising professor and his followers are hard at work on 600 acres of restored tallgrass. One of the forest preserve districts around Chicago is now laying plans for the restoration and care of some 4,000 acres of prairie. Perhaps in our lifetimes we will see the long-sought "prairie parks" at last. And a growing historical interest in Prairie School buildings and public parks promises to restore some of the regional genius the prairies themselves spawned.

For the moment, however, it is the photographs in this exhibit that are the prairies' legacy to us. The earliest ones recorded the last years of the Midwest's untouched beauty, and the newer ones reach in their directness for the prairie spirit, still alive, which gave birth to the Prairie School. They all capture a world which, though changing its vegetative mantle right before the camera's eye, still speaks in its broad horizontal lines of the quiet strength and dignity of America's heartland.

18. Martineau, _op. cit._, p. 178.

Bibliography

Angle, Paul, ed. Prairie State, Chicago: University of Chicago Press, 1968.

Brooks, Allen. The Prairie School: Frank Lloyd Wright and His Contemporaries. New York: W. W. Norton Co., 1972.

Havighurst, Walter, ed. Land of the Long Horizons. New York: Coward-McCann Inc., 1960.

Jensen, Jens. Siftings. Chicago: Ralph Fletcher Seymour, 1939.

Madson, John. Where the Sky Began. Boston: Houghton Mifflin Co., 1982.

Miller, Wilhelm. The Prairie Spirit in Landscape Gardening. Urbana: University of Illinois Press, 1915.

Sandburg, Carl. The Complete Poems of Carl Sandburg. New York: Harcourt, Brace, Jovanovich, Inc., 1969.

Howett, Catherine. "Frank Lloyd Wright and American Residential Landscaping," Landscape 26 (1982), No. 1.

Simonds, Ossian. "Appreciation of Natural Beauty." Second Report of the American Park and Outdoor Art Association. Minneapolis, 1898.

Taft, Lorado. "An American Rural Art Movement." Rural Organization: Proceedings of the Third National County Life Conference. Springfield, Mass., 1920.

Chicago Daily News. May 9, 1943.

Additional Readings on the Midwest Landscape

Angle, Paul M., ed. Prairie State: Impressions of Illinois, 1673-1867, by Travelers and Other Observers. Chicago: University of Chicago Press, 1968.

Babcock, C. Merton. The American Frontier: A Social and Literary Record. New York: Holt, Rinehart and Winston, Inc., 1965.

Bray, Robert C. Rediscoveries: Literature and Place in Illinois. Urbana: University of Illinois Press, 1982.

Brockway, Wallace and Winer, Bart Keith, eds. Homespun America. New York: Simon and Schuster, 1958.

Bryant, William Cullen. Letters of a Traveller, or, Notes of Things Seen In Europe and America. New York: G.P. Putnam, 1850.

Buckingham, Joseph H. Illinois as Lincoln Knew It: A Boston Record of a Trip in 1847. Springfield, Ill.: Harry E. Pratt, 1938.

Derleth, August. New Poetry Out of Wisconsin. Sauk City, Wisc.: Stanton and Lee, 1969.

Flanagan, John T. America Is West: An Anthology of Middlewestern Life and Literature. Minneapolis: University of Minnesota Press, 1945.

Frederick, John T., ed. Stories from the Midland. New York: Alfred A. Knopf, 1924.

______. Out of the Midwest: A Collection of Present-Day Writing. New York: McGraw-Hill, 1944.

Gebhard, Fred. Illinois As It Is. Chicago: Keen and Lee, 1857.

Greenberg, David B., comp. and ed. Land That Our Fathers Plowed. Norman: University of Oklahoma Press, 1969.

Kilpatrick, Thomas L. and Hoshiko, Patsy-Rose, eds. Illinois! Illinois! An Annotated Bibliography of Fiction. New Jersey: The Scarecrow Press, 1979.

Larrick, Nancy, ed. Room for Me and a Mountain Lion: Poetry of Open Space. New York: M. Evans and Co., 1974.

Martineau, Harriet. Society in America. London: Saunders and Otley, 1837.

Nemanic, Gerald, ed. A Bibliographical Guide to Midwestern Literature. Iowa City: University of Iowa Press, 1981.

Schoolcraft, Henry R. Travels in the Central Portions of the Mississippi Valley, Comprising Observations and Its Mineral Geography, Internal Resources, and Aboriginal Population. New York: Collins and Hannay, 1825.

Steele, Elizabeth. A Summer's Journey in the West. New York: John S. Taylor and Co., 1841.

Stibitz, Earle, ed. Illinois Poets: A Selection. Carbondale: Southern Illinois University Press, 1968.

Stryk, Lucien, ed. Heartland: Poets of the Midwest. DeKalb: Northern Illinois University Press, 1967.

______. Heartland II: Poets of the Midwest. DeKalb: Northern Illinois University Press, 1975.

Wimberly, Lowry C., ed. Mid-Country: Writings from the Heart of America. New York: Thomas Crowell, 1945.

Woods, John. Two Years' Residence on the English Prairie. Edited by Paul Angle. Chicago: R.R. Donnelley and Sons Co., 1968.

Gohlke, Frank
Grain Elevator and Plowed Fields, Wellington, Kansas, 1973
silver gelatin print, 299 x 299mm.
Lent by the photographer.

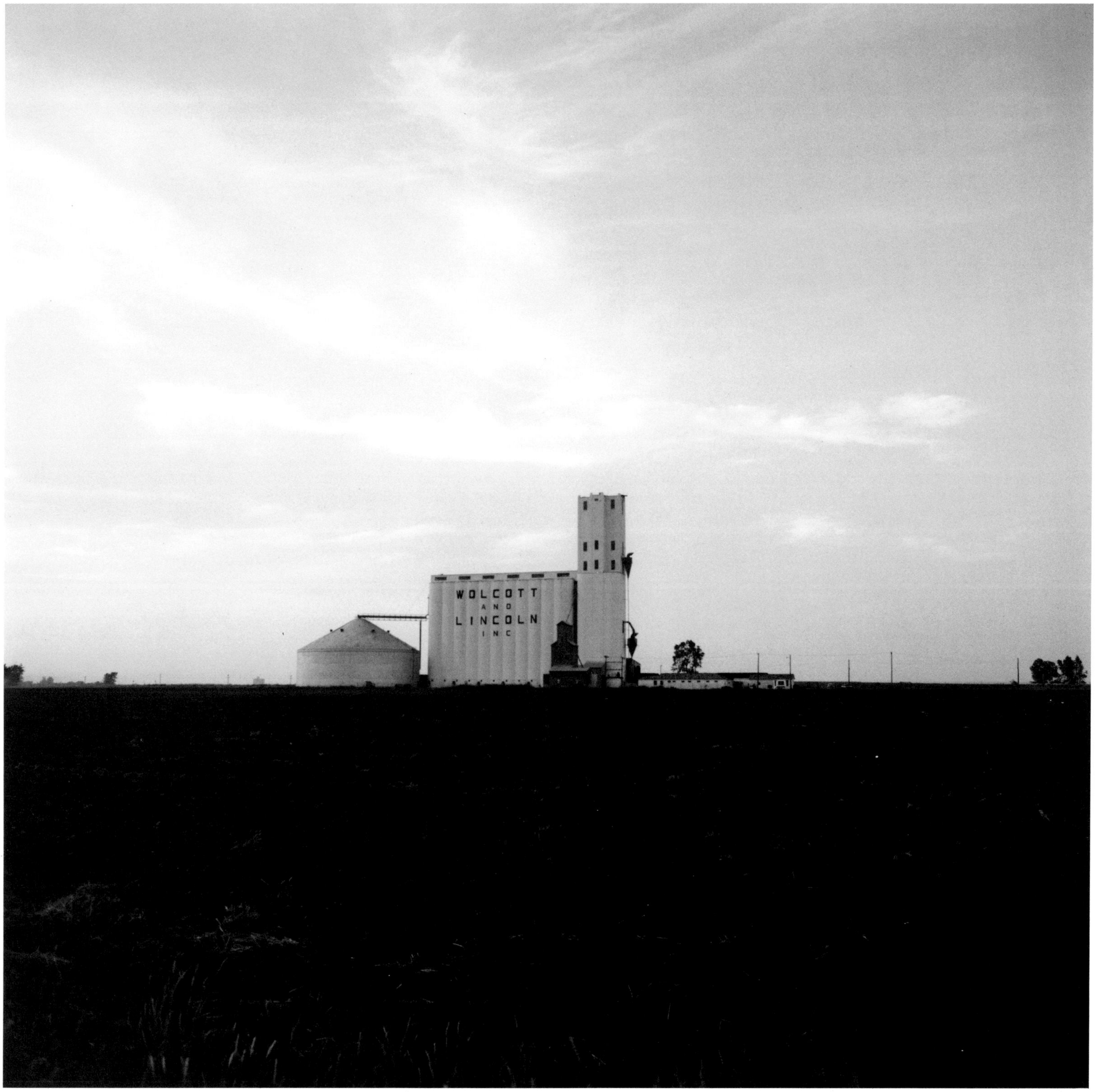

HOW THIS LAND WAS FORMED

by Louise B. Young

The fertile agricultural heartland of America is a vast plain extending across the north central states—from eastern Ohio through eastern Nebraska and the Dakotas—from the Great Lakes to the Ohio River in the east and down into Oklahoma in the west. In this central lowland many favorable factors have come together, creating the largest stretch of prime farmland in the world.

The climate in these latitudes provides a generous growing season. Precipitation is ample, watering the crops and restoring the water table. The top soil is rich in nutrients, soft and friable; so it is easy to cultivate. And almost everywhere the topography is flat or very gently rolling. The unique characteristics of this prairie land were more than 500 million years in the making.

As far back in time as we can trace the earth's history in any detail, this piece of the earth's crust has been part of a relatively stable land mass, the center of the North American craton. It is flanked on the east and west by "mobile belts," bands of the planet's surface that have undergone much greater upheaval and change. The mobile belt in the east created the Appalachian Mountains and the western mobile belt gave birth to the Rocky Mountains, the Sierra Nevada and Cascade ranges. From the middle of the Cambrian Period, about 520 million years ago when shelled organisms had begun to multiply in the ancient seas, until 60 million years ago this land was occupied for very long periods by epeiric seas, wide shallow bodies of water similar to the Bahama Banks of today. Across the bottom of these seas, layer after layer of mud became compacted into shale. And carbonates, derived from the aquatic organisms, formed broad sheets of limestone.

About 500 million years ago mountain building began in the eastern mobile belt and persisted throughout many eons. Now and then the seas retreated from the center of the craton and dry land emerged. But even during those times the smoothing process continued on the low lands as the planet's crust was eroded from the regions of higher elevation, washed down by the rivers, and deposited in the shallow basins. Eventually the seas returned, inundating the land again.

During the Mesozoic Era (from 225 to 65 million years ago) while dinosaurs made their appearance, dominated the earth, and finally died out, great changes continued to occur in the crust of the planet. Continents split and drifted apart, ice ages came and went. But still the central lowlands of North America lay relatively undisturbed.

About 100 million years ago the western mobile belt, known as the Cordillera, began to undergo major tectonic changes. Mountain systems were raised up and eroded again, shedding large volumes of red gravels, sandstone, and shale. By 58 million years ago the last epeiric sea had drained from the continent. All the land was emergent and exposed to the weather. As sediments were stripped from the mountains, carried eastward by streams, and deposited in broad alluvial fans, a plateau of higher elevation was created in the area that is now Montana, eastern Wyoming and Colorado, western Kansas, Nebraska, and the Dakotas. The winds bringing in moisture-laden clouds off the Pacific Ocean flowed from west to east across the continent as they do today. So the western plains region lay in the rain shadow of the mountains and received less precipitation than the land further downwind. It became a semi-arid savannah as it remains today—the short-grass prairies of the Great Plains.

In the meantime the lower flat land in the center of the craton received more abundant precipitation. Alternately washed by showers, swept by winds, the surface sediments were gradually removed from the land, exposing the ancient rocks below. The bedrock across all the central lowlands is very old, dating back 250 million years or more.

Throughout the whole Cenozoic Era, the time when mammals diversified and spread throughout the earth, tectonic changes continued to rock the planet, rearranging the configuration of the ocean basins and the great land masses. But the heartland of America remained quiescent— a broad lowland with relatively gentle profile.

It was not until two million years ago, a date corresponding roughly with the advent of man, that this region underwent a major geologic change as the latest series of ice ages descended on the planet. Glaciers, formed in Canada and Greenland, pushed down across the central lowlands. At its greatest extent the ice covered almost all of the land down to where the Ohio and Missouri rivers now flow. Like giant bulldozers, the heavy ice packs put the finishing touches on the Midwest landscape as they moved south, slicing off the regions of higher elevation and carrying their substance as loose soil, sand, gravel, and assorted boulders. When the ice began to melt in the warmer air, it dropped its load of sediments. This unconsolidated soil filled the valleys to greater depths than the high lands, thus evening out the small irregularities in

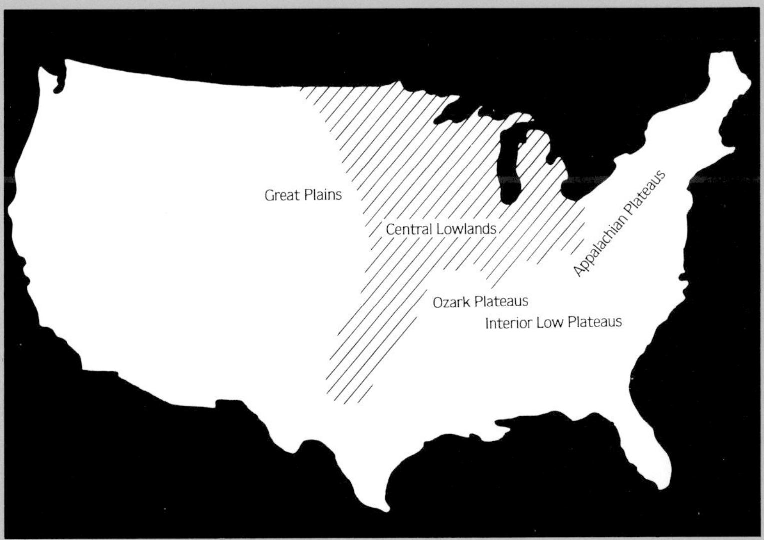

surface contour. A great till plain was created extending over large parts of Ohio, Michigan, Indiana, Wisconsin, and the Dakotas. Where the ice reached its maximum extension and began to retreat, thicker deposits became terminal moraines, low hills that follow the curving contours of the glacial lobes. More hillocks and meandering ridges were created from gravels carried by streams that flowed beneath the ice. These formations added small relief features to an otherwise level terrain.

As the tremendous quantities of ice melted, torrential floods occurred. The waters spilled out over the river banks and carved wide valleys which were periodically covered with mud and sand. When these dried out they were picked up by the wind and scattered as fine dust across thousands of square miles. The lands downwind of the Missouri and Mississippi rivers received the heaviest outfall of this fine "loess." It lies in a thick blanket smoothing the outlines of the landscape across large portions of Illinois, Iowa, Missouri, and Kansas—in some places 30, 50, even 90 feet deep. It forms a soft, richly nutrient agricultural soil which is, however, severely susceptible to erosion. These lands must be farmed with great care to preserve their mantle of loess, the most valuable gift of the ice ages.

The great river systems and large bodies of water that characterize the central lowlands were also shaped by the glaciers. Waters, dammed up by ice, created enormous lakes. The greatest of these was Lake Agassiz, lying in what is now the Red River valley between North Dakota and Minnesota and northward far into Canada. Later the waters retreated, leaving a plain of lake-deposited silt and clay, rich in organic matter. Lake Algonquin, ancestor of the Great Lakes, occupied parts of northern Ohio, Indiana, Michigan, and Wisconsin as well as the present lake basins. Throughout this time the Great Lakes have served as giant reservoirs, helping to maintain the water table and to provide adequate moisture for America's heartland.

Thus many factors have cooperated to produce the finest agricultural land in the world: rain, snow, warm summer days, and immense expanses of rich soil. Where a hundred years ago a sea of flowers stretched from horizon to horizon, now row after row of young corn converge in mathematical precision as far as the eye can see. The views of Midwest prairie land are clean and uncluttered, with a purity of line that reveals the true shape of the earth—not flat but very gently curving where the body of the planet itself meets the sky.

Bibliography

Dott, Robert H. Jr., and Batten, Roger L. Evolution of the Earth. 2d ed. New York: McGraw-Hill, Inc., 1976.

Fenneman, Nevin. Physiography of the Eastern United States. New York and London: McGraw-Hill Book Company, 1938.

Hunt, Charles B. Geology of Soils. San Francisco and London: W.H. Freeman and Co., 1972.

Physiography of the United States. San Francisco and London: W.H. Freeman and Co., 1967.

Photographs in The Exhibition
(Asterisk indicates catalogue illustration)

Adams, Robert
The Pawnee Grasslands, 1973
silver gelatin print, 231 x 297mm.
Lent by the photographer.

*Adams, Robert
Missouri River, Clay County, S.D., 1977
silver gelatin print, 231 x 297mm.
Lent by The Art Institute of Chicago
Restricted gift of Louise Lutz, 1982.138.

Allen, J.C.
Mississippi River at Source, Near Lake Itasca, Minnesota, 1925
silver gelatin print, 115 x 164mm.
Lent by J.C. Allen & Son, Inc., West Lafayette, Indiana.

*Allen, J.C.
Scene in Switzerland County, Indiana, June 1922
silver gelatin print, 115 x 164mm.
Lent by J.C. Allen & Son, Inc., West Lafayette, Indiana.

*Allen, J.C.
Scene from Elevator Near Earl Park, Indiana, July 1927
silver gelatin print, 115 x 164mm.
Lent by J.C. Allen & Son, Inc., West Lafayette, Indiana.

*Anonymous
Man Standing in Center of Wheatfield, n.d. WHi x3 39564
silver gelatin print, 158 x 206mm.
Lent by the Iconographic Collections, State Historical Society of Wisconsin, Madison, Wisconsin.

*Anonymous
Man on Bluff, Mississippi River, 1930
silver gelatin print, 162 x 112mm.
Lent by Principia College, Elsah, Illinois.

*Anonymous
Two Hundred Twenty-Acre Field, Headed, Stewart Valley, Saskatchewan, c. 1918
silver gelatin print, 62 x 168mm.
Lent by the Minnesota Historical Society, St. Paul, Minnesota.

Anonymous
View of a Farm on the Prairie, North Dakota, c. 1899
silver gelatin print, 124 x 164mm.
Lent by Loyola University of Chicago Archives, Catholic Church Extension Society Records.

Anonymous
The First Train into Ashland, Kansas, 1887
silver gelatin print, 120 x 234mm.
Lent by Loyola University of Chicago Archives, Catholic Church Extension Society Records.

Anonymous
Near Elsah, Illinois, 1930
silver gelatin print, 112 x 162mm.
Lent by Principia College, Elsah, Illinois.

Anonymous
Farm Buildings and Road in Shadow, Field in Sunlight, c. 1942
color photograph, C-print, 119 x 173mm.
Lent by the Regional History Center, Northern Illinois University, DeKalb, Illinois.

Anonymous
Linn County, Iowa (three men in landscape, two holding shotguns, one a handsaw), c. 1870
albumen print, 180 x 230mm.
Lent by the State Historical Society, Iowa State Historical Department, Iowa City, Iowa.

Anonymous
Linn County, Iowa (landscape with farm buildings), c. 1870
albumen print, 180 x 230mm.
Lent by the State Historical Society, Iowa State Historical Department, Iowa City, Iowa.

Anonymous
Olund Farm (northwestern Iowa), c. 1892
silver gelatin print, 154 x 208mm.
Lent by the State Historical Society, Iowa State Historical Department, Iowa City, Iowa.

*Arndt, Tom
Bismarck, North Dakota, 1981
silver gelatin print, 316 x 473mm.
Lent by Henryka Frajlich-Manès.

Arndt, Tom
Farm, North Dakota, 1981
silver gelatin print, 316 x 473mm.
Lent by Henryka Frajlich-Manès.

Arndt, Tom
Outside Bismarck, North Dakota, 1981
silver gelatin print, 316 x 473mm.
Lent by Henryka Frajlich-Manès.

*Bill, Frank
Aerial View, McLean County, Illinois, 1930
silver gelatin print, 124 x 167mm.
Lent by the Bloomington, Illinois, Daily Pantagraph.

Bill, Frank
Aerial View, McLean County, Illinois, 1930
silver gelatin print, 124 x 167mm.
Lent by the Bloomington, Illinois, Daily Pantagraph.

*Boersma, Jay
Northern Indiana, 1973-74
silver gelatin print, 203 x 253mm.
Lent by the photographer.

Boersma, Jay
Northern Indiana, 1973-74
silver gelatin print, 203 x 253mm.
Lent by the photographer.

Brooks Studio, Little Falls, Minnesota
Farm Scene in Morrison County, 1900
silver gelatin print, 161 x 212mm.
Lent by the Minnesota Historical Society, St. Paul, Minnesota.

Calvin, Samuel
Boulders on Open Field, c. 1880
silver gelatin print, 126 x 200mm.
Modern print by James Goodell from a negative in the Calvin Collection, Department of Geology, University of Iowa, Iowa City, Iowa.
Lent by Open Lands Project of Chicago.

Calvin, Samuel
Landscape with Farm House, c. 1880
silver gelatin print, 126 x 200mm.
Modern print by James Goodell from a negative in the Calvin Collection, Department of Geology, University of Iowa, Iowa City, Iowa.
Lent by Open Lands Project of Chicago.

*Cheek, Vernon
Indiana Landscape, 1982
color photograph, C-print, 130 x 166mm.
Lent by the photographer.

Cheek, Vernon
Indiana Landscape, 1980
color photograph, C-print, 96 x 121mm.
Lent by the photographer.

*Cialdella, Gary A.
Landscape, Small Trees and Cornfield Near Berrien Springs, Michigan, 1981
silver gelatin print, 206 x 455mm.
Lent by the photographer.

Cialdella, Gary A.
Fence Row and Plowed Field, Near Decatur, Michigan, 1982
silver gelatin print, 206 x 455mm.
Lent by the photographer.

*Cundill, Will
South Dakota (Girl in Hay Stack), 1915
silver gelatin print, 125 x 175mm.
Modern print by J. Ceronie, Dennett, Muessig & Associates from a negative in the collection of the Iowa State Historical Society, Iowa City, Iowa.
Lent by Open Lands Project of Chicago.

*Dahl, Andrew
Workers with Farm Tools, c. 1873 (WHi (D31) 172)
albumen stereograph, 124 x 201mm.
Print by Elizabeth Chilsen and Lorraine Davis from a negative in the Iconographic Collections, State Historical Society of Wisconsin, Madison, Wisconsin, from paper provided by the Chicago Albumen Works.

*Dahl, Andrew
Workers with Farm Tools, Boy Facing Camera, c. 1873 (WHi (D31) 174)
albumen stereograph, 124 x 201mm.
Print by Elizabeth Chilsen and Lorraine Davis from a negative in the Iconographic Collections, State Historical Society of Wisconsin, Madison, Wisconsin, from paper provided by the Chicago Albumen Works.

Dahl, Andrew
Landscape near Madison, Wisconsin, c. 1873 (WHi (D31) 107)
albumen stereograph, 124 x 201mm.
Print by Elizabeth Chilsen and Lorraine Davis from a negative in the Iconographic Collections, State Historical Society of Wisconsin, Madison, Wisconsin, from paper provided by the Chicago Albumen Works.

Davis, Keith F.
River Front Park, Kansas City, winter 1982
silver gelatin print, 194 x 243mm.
Lent by the photographer.

*Davis, Keith F.
Field, Weston, Missouri, spring 1982
silver gelatin print, 194 x 243mm.
Lent by the photographer.

*Davis, Stephen
Clay County, Minnesota, 1981
silver gelatin print, 228 x 228mm.
Lent by the photographer.

Davis, Stephen
Grant County, Minnesota, 1982
silver gelatin print, 228 x 228mm.
Lent by the photographer.

Deschamps, Francois
Landscape with Fisherman, 1977
color photograph, C-print, 203 x 305mm.
Lent by the photographer.

*Deschamps, Francois
Landscape with Red Tree, 1979
color photograph, C-print, 203 x 305mm.
Lent by the photographer.

Detroit Photographic Company
Iowa, c. 1898
cyanotype, 190 x 240mm.
Lent by the Library of Congress, Washington, D.C.

Detroit Photographic Company
Illinois, c. 1898
cyanotype, 190 x 240mm.
Lent by the Library of Congress, Washington, D.C.

*Enyeart, James
Riley County, No. 3, c. 1970
silver gelatin print, 254 x 327 mm.
Lent by the Spencer Museum of Art, The University of Kansas, Lawrence, Kansas.

Enyeart, James
Sherman County, No. 1, c. 1970
silver gelatin print, 260 x 254 mm.
Lent by the Spencer Museum of Art, The University of Kansas, Lawrence, Kansas.

Evans, Terry
Fent's Prairie, Salina, Kansas, 1980
color photograph, C-print, 229 x 229mm.
Lent by the photographer.

*Evans, Terry
Konza Prairie Near Manhattan, Kansas, 1982
color photograph, C-print, 229 x 229mm.
Lent by the photographer.

Evans, Terry
Chase County, Kansas, 1979
color photograph, C-print, 229 x 229mm.
Lent by the photographer.

*Ferguson, Larry
Polled Herefords, Near Niobrara, Nebraska, 1981
chlorobromide silver print, 215 x 305mm.
Lent by the photographer.

Ferguson, Larry
Cattle Call, 1978
silver gelatin print, 182 x 305mm.
Lent by the photographer.

*Fisher, Anna
Calhoun County, Illinois, c. 1903
silver gelatin print, 115 x 165mm.
Lent by Pike County Historical Society, Illinois.

Fisher, Anna
Diamond Island, Calhoun County, Illinois, c. 1903
silver gelatin print, 113 x 166mm.
Lent by Pike County Historical Society, Illinois.

Fisher, Anna
High Water, Calhoun County, Illinois, c. 1903
silver gelatin print, 118 x 165mm.
Lent by Pike County Historical Society, Illinois.

Flick, Robbert
Sequential Views, "Chicago Forest Preserve," 1982
silver gelatin prints, 395 x 544mm.
Lent by the photographer and Tortue Gallery of Santa Monica, California.

*Flick, Robbert
Sequential Views, "North of Kankakee, Illinois," 1981
silver gelatin prints, 354 x 544mm.
Lent by the photographer and Tortue Gallery of Santa Monica, California.

*Neal Fox Studio, Thief River Falls, Minnesota
Combines on the Frank Keine Farm, Marshall County, c. 1960
silver gelatin print, 195 x 244mm.
Lent by the Minnesota Historical Society, St. Paul, Minnesota.

*Gardner, Alexander
View Near Fort Harker, Kansas, 1867
albumen print, 149 x 202mm.
Lent by the Missouri Historical Society, St. Louis, Missouri.

*Gardner, Alexander
Overlooking Lawrence and the Kansas River, 1867
albumen print, 150 x 203mm.
Lent by the Missouri Historical Society, St. Louis, Missouri.

Gardner, Alexander
On the Great Plains, in Kansas, Near Monument, 1867
albumen print, 150 x 202mm.
Lent by the Missouri Historical Society, St. Louis, Missouri.

*Gesell, Gerhard
Near Alma, Wisconsin, c. 1890
silver gelatin print, 188 x 246mm.
Lent by the Iconographic Collections, State Historical Society of Wisconsin, Madison, Wisconsin.

*Gohlke, Frank
Grain Elevator and Plowed Fields, Wellington, Kansas, 1973
silver gelatin print, 299 x 299mm.
Lent by the photographer.

*Gohlke, Frank
Farm Yard Near Houston, Minnesota, 1977
silver gelatin print, 279 x 347mm.
Lent by the photographer.

Gohlke, Frank
Looking East Across Mississippi River from Garvin Heights, Winona, Minnesota, 1977
silver gelatin print, 278 x 350mm.
Lent by the photographer.

*Hesler, Alexander
Galena, Illinois, 1852
daguerreotype, 166 x 216mm.
Lent by the Iconographic Collections, State Historical Society of Wisconsin, Madison, Wisconsin.

*Hickman, C.A.
South Dakota Landscape with Children, c. 1890
silver gelatin print, 52 x 176mm.
Lent by Robert Adams.

Hickman, C.A.
South Dakota Landscape with Buggy, c. 1890
silver gelatin print, 52 x 176mm.
Lent by Robert Adams.

*Hime, H.L.
The Prairie, on the Banks of the Red River, Looking South, September-October, 1858
albumen print, 133 x 170mm.
Lent by Notman Photographic Archives, McCord Museum, McGill University, Montreal, Quebec, Canada.

*Hime, H.L.
Tents on the Prairie, West of the Settlement, September-October, 1858
albumen print, 133 x 170mm.
Lent by Notman Photographic Archives, McCord Museum, McGill University, Montreal, Quebec, Canada.

Hotchkiss, Duane
Grove of Trees, c. 1930
silver gelatin print, 116 x 169mm.
Lent by the Kankakee County, Illinois, Historical Society Museum, Photo Collection.

Iversen, Earl
From Deep Creek Road, Flint Hills, Kansas, 1979
silver gelatin print, 218 x 328mm.
Lent by the photographer.

*Iversen, Earl
Flint Hills South of Emporia, Cattle Pens Area, Interstate 35, 1979
silver gelatin print, 218 x 328mm.
Lent by the photographer.

Johnson, Michael
Watercourse, 1976
silver gelatin print, 215 x 313mm.
On loan to the Art Institute of Chicago from Jack and Roberta Jaffe.

*Johnson, Michael
Road, Wacker, 1978
silver gelatin print, 228 x 319mm.
On loan to the Art Institute of Chicago from Jack and Roberta Jaffe.

*Johnson, W.D.
Man Sitting by Sink Hole (Kansas), 1897
silver gelatin print, 120 x 170mm.
Modern print by Rod Mettler from a negative in the collection of the U.S. Geological Survey. Lent by Open Lands Project of Chicago.

Johnson, W.D.
Kansas Landscape with Abandoned Buildings, 1897
silver gelatin print, 120 x 170mm.
Modern print by Rod Mettler from a negative in the collection of the U.S. Geological Survey.
Lent by Open Lands Project of Chicago.

Klipper, Stuart
Corn Field, U.S. 169, North of Ft. Dodge, Iowa, 1982
color photograph, C-print, 180 x 578mm.
Lent by the photographer.

*Klipper, Stuart
Farm with Elsie the Cow on the Barn, Humboldt County, Iowa, 1982
color photograph, C-print, 180 x 578mm.
Lent by the photographer.

*Lane, Frank
Fisherman, Reflection, c. 1896
silver gelatin print, 76 x 100mm.
Lent by the Momence (Illinois) Historical Society.

Lane, Frank
Fisherman, c. 1896
silver gelatin print, 78 x 99mm.
Lent by the Momence (Illinois) Historical Society.

Lane, Frank
Landscape with Cow, c. 1896
silver gelatin print, 97 x 117mm.
Lent by the Momence (Illinois) Historical Society.

*Lazar, Arthur
Ohio, 1978
platinum print, 120 x 170mm.
Lent by the photographer.

Lazar, Arthur
Ohio, (trees), 1978
platinum print 120 x 170 mm.
Lent by the photographer.

McFarland, Lawrence
Cow on Pole, Kansas, c. 1976
silver gelatin print, 265 x 430mm.
Lent by the photographer.

*McFarland, Lawrence
Near Linsborg, Kansas, 1976
silver gelatin print, 265 x 430mm.
Lent by the photographer.

*McFarland, Lawrence
Wheatfield, 1976
silver gelatin print, 265 x 430mm.
Lent by the photographer.

McKinney, Rhondal
Illinois Landscape (wheat), 1982
silver gelatin print, 190 x 240mm.
Lent by the photographer.

*McKinney, Rhondal
Illinois Landscape, 1982
silver gelatin print, 190 x 240mm.
Lent by the photographer.

*McKinney, Rhondal
Illinois Landscape, 1979
silver gelatin print, 190 x 240mm.
Lent by the photographer.

*Morris, Wright
House in Winter, Near Lincoln, 1941
silver gelatin print, 192 x 241mm.
Lent by The Weston Gallery, Inc., Carmel, California.

*Morris, Wright
Abandoned Farm, Western Nebraska, 1941
silver gelatin print, 192 x 241mm.
Lent by The Weston Gallery, Inc., Carmel, California.

Paul, Kathryn
La Rue Pine Hills, 1982
silver gelatin print, 230 x 327mm.
Lent by the photographer.

***Paul, Kathryn**
Richard at Lusk Creek, 1982
silver gelatin print, 233 x 326mm.
Lent by the photographer.

***Pennell, Joseph Judd**
Tom Flannagan's Monument, 1898
silver gelatin print, 183 x 224mm.
Modern print by Jon Blumb
from a negative in the Kansas Collection,
University of Kansas, Lawrence, Kansas.
Lent by Open Lands Project of Chicago.

Pennell, Joseph Judd
Harger County Scenery, 1902
silver gelatin print, 125 x 175mm.
Modern print by Jon Blumb
from a negative in the Kansas Collection,
University of Kansas, Lawrence, Kansas.
Lent by Open Lands Project of Chicago.

Perkins, Harvey J.
Near Phillips, Wisconsin, 1895
(WHi (H44) 16)
albumen print, 166 x 216mm.
Print by Elizabeth Chilsen and Lorraine Davis
from a negative in the Iconographic
Collections, State Historical Society
of Wisconsin, Madison, Wisconsin.
Albumen paper provided by the Chicago
Albumen Works.

Perkins, Harvey J.
Man Standing in Field, 1895
(WHi (H44) 92)
albumen print, 166 x 216mm.
Print by Elizabeth Chilsen and Lorraine Davis
from a negative in the Iconographic
Collections, State Historical Society
of Wisconsin, Madison, Wisconsin.
Albumen paper provided by the Chicago
Albumen Works.

Persons, W.C.
Field of Wheat Shocks, c. 1925
silver gelatin print, 192 x 244mm.
Lent by the Missouri Historical Society,
St. Louis, Missouri.

***Persons, W.C.**
Threshing Scene, c. 1920
silver gelatin print, 186 x 241mm.
Lent by the Missouri Historical Society,
St. Louis, Missouri.

***Plasko, Nancy Sparrow**
Restored Prairie, Big Stone
Wildlife Refuge, November 1980
silver gelatin print, 243 x 305mm.
Lent by the photographer.

Plasko, Nancy Sparrow
Unplowed Prairie Quarter Section,
Big Stone County, June 1981
silver gelatin print, 243 x 305mm.
Lent by the photographer.

***Plowden, David**
Nuclear Generating Station,
Sillman Valley, Illinois, 1981
silver gelatin print, 241 x 325mm.
Lent by the photographer.

Plowden, David
Farm, Will County, Illinois, 1981
silver gelatin print, 237 x 325mm.
Lent by the photographer.

***Plowden, David**
Near Peotone, Illinois, 1981
silver gelatin print, 259 x 308mm.
Lent by the photographer.

***Ridgeway, Robert**
Southern Illinois, Woman in White Dress,
c. 1885
silver gelatin print, 115 x 167mm.
Lent by the Chicago Academy of Sciences.

Ridgeway, Robert
Southern Illinois, Tree, c. 1885
silver gelatin print, 178 x 118mm.
Lent by the Chicago Academy of Sciences.

Ridgeway, Robert
Southern Illinois, Cypress Trunks, c. 1885
silver gelatin print, 119 x 178mm.
Lent by the Chicago Academy of Sciences.

***Robinson, F.N.**
The Only Cyclone Ever Photographed
(Miner County, South Dakota),
August 28, 1884
albumen print, 104 x 151mm.
Lent by the South Dakota State Historical
Society, Pierre, South Dakota.

***Rothstein, Arthur**
Iowa, 1937
(LC34 29420)
silver gelatin print, 179 x 240mm.
From a negative in the collection
of the Prints and Photographs Division,
Library of Congress, Washington, D.C.
Lent by Open Lands Project of Chicago.

***Schwarm, Larry**
Cornfield near Colby, Kansas, c. 1975
color photograph, C-print, 217 x 319mm.
Lent by the photographer.

Schwarm, Larry
Northwestern Kansas, c. 1976
color photograph, C-print, 217 x 320mm.
Lent by the photographer.

***Sinsabaugh, Art**
Midwest Landscape #24, 1961
silver gelatin print, 67 x 490mm.
Lent by Edwynn Houk Gallery, Chicago.

Sinsabaugh, Art
Midwest Landscape #60, 1961
silver gelatin print, 112 x 490mm.
Lent by Edwynn Houk Gallery, Chicago.

***Sinsabaugh, Art**
Midwest Landscape #78, 1963
silver gelatin print, 121 x 494mm.
Lent by the Art Institute of Chicago,
Restricted gift of the Joseph and Helen
Regenstein Foundation, 1963.750.

Sweet, Louis D.
Lake Pepin near Lake City, Minnesota,
1904
silver gelatin print, 190 x 240mm.
Lent by the Minnesota Historical Society,
St. Paul, Minnesota.

***Vanderbilt, Paul**
Field Road Near
Black Earth, Wisconsin, 1962
silver gelatin print, 204 x 333mm.
Lent by the Art Institute of Chicago,
Gift of the photographer and the State
Historical Society of Wisconsin, 1965.904.

***Vanderbilt, Paul**
Near Coon Valley, Wisconsin, 1962
silver gelatin print, 215 x 300mm.
Lent by the Art Institute of Chicago,
Gift of the photographer and the State
Historical Society of Wisconsin, 1965.905.

Vanderbilt, Paul
Hillsboro, Wisconsin Vicinity, 1965
(WHi (X2) 16087)
silver gelatin print, 133 x 230mm.
Lent by the Iconographics Collections,
State Historical Society of Wisconsin,
Madison, Wisconsin.

***Woods, Lucia**
Ivar's Pond, 1972
silver gelatin print, 202 x 305mm.
Lent by The Art Institute of Chicago,
Mary and Leigh Block Fund for Acquisitions,
1975.579.